国家社会科学基金项目
“香港回归后的政治话语及其建构模式研究”（10CYY011）
教育部人文社科重点研究基地项目
“跨文化语篇能力研究”（16JJD740006）
研究成果

华南师范大学学术出版基金资助出版

语言服务书系·社会语言学研究

华南师范大学外国语言文化学院学术文库

# 话语策略与身份建构

## 基于香港回归前后
## 政府施政报告的研究

王加林 著

# Discursive Strategies and Identity Construction

## A Study Based on the PAs of the
## HK Governments Pre- and Post-Transition

暨南大学出版社
JINAN UNIVERSITY PRESS

中国·广州

**图书在版编目（CIP）数据**

话语策略与身份建构：基于香港回归前后政府施政报告的研究 = Discursive Strategies and Identity Construction：A Study Based on the PAs of the HK Governments Pre- and Post-Transition：英文 / 王加林著．—广州：暨南大学出版社，2017.12
（语言服务书系．社会语言学研究）
ISBN 978 - 7 - 5668 - 2298 - 7

Ⅰ.①话…　Ⅱ.①王…　Ⅲ.①语言—关系—政治—研究—英文　Ⅳ.①H0 - 05

中国版本图书馆 CIP 数据核字（2017）第 321724 号

**话语策略与身份建构：基于香港回归前后政府施政报告的研究**
HUAYU CELUE YU SHENFEN JIANGOU：JIYU XIANGGANG HUIGUI QIANHOU ZHENGFU SHIZHENG BAOGAO DE YANJIU
**著　者：王加林**

..........................................................................................

**出 版 人：** 徐义雄
**策　　划：** 杜小陆　刘　晶
**责任编辑：** 杜小陆　李　鹏
**责任校对：** 苏　洁
**责任印制：** 汤慧君　周一丹

**出版发行：** 暨南大学出版社（510630）
**电　　话：** 总编室（8620）85221601
营销部（8620）85225284　85228291　85228292（邮购）
**传　　真：**（8620）85221583（办公室）　85223774（营销部）
**网　　址：** http：//www. jnupress. com
**排　　版：** 广州良弓广告有限公司
**印　　刷：** 佛山市浩文彩色印刷有限公司
**开　　本：** 787mm × 960mm　1/16
**印　　张：** 11.75
**字　　数：** 230 千
**版　　次：** 2017 年 12 月第 1 版
**印　　次：** 2017 年 12 月第 1 次
**定　　价：** 39.80 元

# 序

王加林博士的专著《话语策略与身份建构——基于香港回归前后政府施政报告的研究》基于其博士论文相关的研究以及后续的成果整合而成，为社会语言学学术园地又增添了一道景色；在祝贺其即将付梓之时，应约作序，我想还是从该著作的题目讲起，说说话语与身份有什么关系。

讲起身份问题，首先浮现在我脑海的是发生在广外校园里的一则趣闻：一位外籍教师（华裔母亲）带着小宝宝在校园里散步，碰上了同事的太太也带着小宝宝出来遛弯，于是亲热地凑上前去，教自己的小宝宝打招呼："小弟弟好!"对方的直接反应是"你们的是哪个月出生的啊?"当对方发现先打招呼的小朋友是同年晚三个月出生时，马上纠正说："不对，我们的是哥哥，要说'哥哥好'。"事后，那位华裔母亲感叹道，忘了年龄辈序在汉语文化中有这么重要。这件趣事也许从一个侧面说明，我们每一个人的某种身份都是一定的社会文化给予并且通过话语加以固化（建构）的。

上述趣事只是日常生活中关涉身份的一个例子，而我们每一个人一生中随着人生经历的转折或受社会变迁的影响，身份亦随之发生变化，譬如，一个人从"儿子"成长为"父亲"，一个人通过移民将自己变成"某国人"……。对于这些变化人们常常习以为常，也不会特别在意其中所涉及的社会文化或者社会政治因素。其实，使用语言（话语）体现（建构）身份的现象无时不存在于每一个人的生活之中，小到在温馨的家庭里刚当上父亲的人教小宝宝称自己"爸爸"，大至人们在一定的社会政治场合大声喊出"我是中国人"，这些都是使用话语建构身份的现象。

20 世纪末，香港回归祖国是中华民族历史上的重大事件。这一社会变迁意味着从 1997 年 7 月 1 日起，香港人可以挺起腰杆，将自己的英国海外公民身份变成堂堂正正的中国人（中华人民共和国公民）身份。对于不同社会背景的亲历者，这种身份的骤然变化有着截然不同的意涵，其中不乏涉及社会、政治、社会心理诸多的因素。这种翻天覆地的社会变迁及所伴随的香港人特殊身份的转变必然会成为社会语言学界关注的话题，因为这其中所涉及的社会政治发展进程，对于开展社会语言学研究，尤其是观察语言与社会互动、话语与身份建构都是极其难得的机缘。

在这种社会变迁的语境下，王加林博士给香港人身份建构的话语策略研究找到一个很好的切入点，通过比较回归前的港英政府（1986—1996 年）和回归后的香港特别行政区政府（1997—2008 年）在前后 22 个年度所发布的政府施政报告文本，集中探讨及对比代表不同主权国家的港英政府/香港特别行政区政府对香港人身份的话语建构策略，以揭示社会政治变迁与身份话语建构之间的共变关系，以及话语及权力如何影响社会意识、建构人们的社会身份，这具有深刻的社会语言学价值及社会实践意义。

该项研究在研究方法上综合运用社会语言学，尤其是社会建构理论和批评话语分析的理论及方法，从宏观策略和微观策略两个层面揭示社会身份建构过程中话语策略如何服务于不同政治目的、话语策略在身份建构中如何发挥重要的社会符号功能以及社会身份话语建构的策略如何服务于政权的建设以及引导社会的发展。此项研究成果在理论和实践上为研究话语与身份建构的关系提供了新的路径，对社会语言学视角的社会身份建构理论做出了贡献，在研究实践层面也做出了很好的示范，值得向关注社会语言学发展的同仁，尤其是青年学者隆重推荐。

上述序言始于日常生活里的小故事，试图以小道理见大道理。至此，小道理不一定已说清楚，但至于大道理，更不必赘言，还是留给该专著去讲述、留给读者自己去发现了。

是为序。

2017 年 6 月 6 日

于广东外语外贸大学

# 前　言

身份研究近年来吸引了包括语言学、心理学、人类学、社会学等多个学科领域众多研究者的关注。身份是个体出于对特定社会群体的认可，调整自己的利益、价值观与信仰，以便和该社会群体保持一致（Ivanic，1998），或是对特定群体的不认可，以此疏离及否定该群体的方法，是“自我”与“他人”的对照，可以通过关系来界定。因此，身份是社会交往和社会关系的产物，由包括语篇实践在内的各种具体协商过程所建构（Berger & Luchman，1967；Burr，2003）；它不是固定不变的，而是经常变动的、多面的（Woodward，1997；Martin，1997；Ainsorth & Hardy，2004；王加林、贺显斌，2012）。

语言不仅是人们认识世界的工具，而且是社会的产物和社会现实的有机组成部分。对社会变迁和话语构建的研究表明，语言与社会存在共变关系：语言变化反映出社会现实的变化，语言也参与社会现实（包括身份、社会关系等）的塑造。话语作为语言的具体应用形式之一，自然也具有身份建构的功能（Burr，2003；De Fina，2006；项蕴华，2009），成为“建构‘想象共同体’（imagined community）的重要工具”（Martin，1995）。通过话语分析可以发现话语作者如何通过不同的话语策略使人们认同或疏离某个社会群体的利益和价值观，从而建构出“自我”与“他人”不同的身份。

关于语言与身份塑造之间的关系，多数研究证实身份可以通过语言得到建构。香港政府施政报告是香港最重要的政治语篇，最能体现香港社会机构的“话语秩序”，即政府对某一社会群体身份的理论描述（项蕴华，2009），具有建构香港身份的重要功能。本书基于22个年度的两个香港政府施政报告的分析——1986年至1996年的港英政府和1997年至2008年的香港特区政府，探讨及对比香港身份的话语构建。通过应用批评性话语分析的研究方法，特别是Wodak（1999）的话语历史方法和van Dijk（1997）的社会认知方法，试图利用相关理论来研究两个香港政府在施政报告里对香港身份的话语建构，以揭示社会政治变迁与话语及身份话语建构之间的共变关系，以及话语策略如何影响社会意识。

本书研究框架包括宏观话语策略和微观话语策略，前者侧重于话语的内容，后者侧重于话语建构身份的语言形式。在本书中宏观话语策略进一步划分为对施政报告中涉及的三个方面的内容分析，以及有助于建构香港身份的主题分析。宏观话语策略分析结果表明，经济、政治和文化建构了香港内在的同一性和独特性；主题分析表明，回归前施政报告往往将中国内地建构为外群体（out-group），而回归后的施政报告将中国内地建构为内群体（in-group）。微观话语策略是从指示策略、修辞策略和互文性策略这三个角度，试图阐述施政报告如何通过这些微观话语策略建构内群体的正面形象和外群体的负面形象，即回归前的负面的中国形象和回归后的正面的中国形象。

本书所使用的批评性话语分析结合了 Wodak（1999）的话语历史方法和 van Dijk（1997）的社会认知方法。根据 Wodak 的话语历史方法，本书从历时性和共时性处理语料，并从不同层次的背景分析讨论。van Dijk 认为意识形态是社会认知的基本形式且话语分析即意识形态的分析，意识形态之两极为正面的内群体和负面的外群体。因此本书采用了两步骤的分析方法：首先是建构内群体和外群体，然后是给不同群体贴上标值——正面与负面。此两步骤分别对应了分析框架内的宏观策略和微观策略。

本书最终阐明了身份的话语可建构性及随社会政治变迁的身份可变性。本书的主要发现如下：回归前香港人的身份在施政报告里被建构为在英国统治下的香港人，强调其“国际性”；回归后香港人的身份在施政报告里被建构为中国的香港人，强调其“中国性”。

本书的价值可以概括为：①从理论层面提出二分法的分析框架——宏观话语策略和微观话语策略的区分，以及两步骤的分析方法，利用意识形态的两极（正面内群体和负面外群体），分析及论证了该框架对身份研究及话语策略分析的可适用性；②结合 Wodak 的话语历史方法和 van Dijk 的社会认知方法的批判性话语分析，开创性地把语言学、政治学、修辞学的相关知识运用于语料分析中，延续了批判性话语的跨学科性的特点，揭示了如何运用语言策略建构不同的身份，使话语中的身份建构成为值得关注的领域；③通过对回归前后施政报告中话语策略的对比分析，揭示语言如何利用话语策略在身份建构中发挥重要的社会符号功能，以及身份话语建构的策略如何服务于政权的建设并引导社会的发展，为政治话语提供理论指导；④本书在理论上和实践上进一步丰富了香港人身份的研究，为语言与身份研究提供一个新视角，同时亦从社会语言学角度丰富并推进身份理论研究。

本书是国家社科基金青年项目“香港回归后政治话语及其建构模式研究”（10CYY011）和广东外语外贸大学教育部人文社科重点研究基地项目“当代中国社会变迁与话语建构”（2009JJD740006）的阶段性成果。书中第二章至第六章的实践研究内容大多已在知名期刊上发表过，在成书的过程中进行了适度修改。

本书的最终出版与我在广东外语外贸大学文科基地完成博士学位期间的学习和研究是分不开的。在此，我首先要感谢的是我的导师陈建平教授，无论是在读博期间还是完成博士论文之后，陈老师在学术研究上一直对我进行耐心细致的指导，帮助我理清课题思路和开拓研究视角，使我最终完成了博士论文，成功申报了国家社科基金项目。可以说，没有陈老师的帮助和指导，本书不可能取得目前的成果。

感谢福建师范大学外国语学院的尤泽顺教授，作为同门，尤老师开阔了我的研究视野，给我提出各种参考意见，每当我遇到学术问题总能通过他得到解答，每次与他的讨论和交流总让我获益匪浅，是他带领我走进科研项目的大门。感谢本项目的参与人，西南大学外语学院的杨竹博士、广东工业大学外语学院的李玉坤博士、广东外语外贸大学的韩艳梅博士、广州大学外语学院的梁凤娟博士。感谢他们的鼓励和启迪让我在这条路上坚持下来。

感谢华南师范大学外文学院领导和同事对我的支持和鼓励，尤其是主管科研的领导谷红丽教授和张萍教授等。感谢外文学院出版基金为本书的出版提供了资助。感谢暨南大学出版社编辑、校对，他们对学术质量的重视、高涨的工作热情和超乎想象的工作效率使本书能够按计划出版。

最后，我要感谢我的丈夫、孩子、家人和好友，在他们的照顾、关怀、鼓励之下我才能完成此研究。此书的出版是对他们辛勤付出的最好回报。

王加林<br>2017 年 5 月

# Contents

# 缩略词表

BDTC：British Dependent Territories Citizen
BL：Basic Law
BNO：British National (Overseas)
CCP：Chinese Communist Party
CDA：Critical Discourse Analysis
CE：Chief Executive
CEPA：Closer Economic Partnership Arrangement
CFA：the Court of Final Appeal
CL：Critical Linguistics
CPG：Central People's Government
DA：Discourse Analysis
HK：Hong Kong
HKSAR：Hong Kong Special Administrative Region
JD：Joint Declaration
NPCSC：Standing Committee of National People's Congress
PA：Policy Address
PRD：Pearl River Delta
PWC：Preliminary Working Committee
SFL：Systemic Functional Linguistics

# Chapter 1  Introduction

## 1.1  Scope of the study

One of the major concerns in sociolinguistics is social identity, the attraction of which lies in its being a problematic and complex concept insomuch as we recognize it as non-fixed, non-rigid and always being constructed and reconstructed in discourses. Identity research has attracted the attention of researchers from different fields, including linguistics, psychology, anthropology and sociology. An identity is the identification of or alienation from a particular social group (Ivanic, 1998). Language is the product of society and an organic part of social reality. Studies on social change and discourse have shown that there is covariant relationship between language and society, i. e., language reflects social changes (inclusive of identity changes) and social changes are constructed through language use. Discourse, as one of the language forms, has the function of identity construction (Burr, 2003; De Fina, 2006; Xiang, 2009).

This study bases its research of language and identity on a corpus of 22 yearly Hong Kong PAs spanning from 1986 to 2008 in an attempt to uncover the co-variation between socio-political change and the discursive construction of HK identity with an analytical framework generated from the theory of CDA (Critical Discourse Analysis). Hong Kong governments' Policy Address is one of the most important political discourses, which can reflect "institutional discourse order" of Hong Kong, and plays a most important role in the construction of Hong Kong identity.

The 1997 Transition of Hong Kong sovereignty from Britain to the People's Republic of China (PRC) was an epoch-setting event for the Chinese nation in history, and ever since, Hong Kong has been a Special Administrative Region (HKSAR, short for Hong Kong Special Administrative Region) under the sovereignty of the PRC Government for so long but differs from Mainland China in its political system. However, "the real transition has been complex, subtle and profound... this is because the real transition is about identity and not sovereignty" (Yeung, 1998; Chan, 2002). The transition of sovereignty leads to the change of the identity of the Hong Kong people who, according to the previous Common Law of the British Colonial HK Government, having been British citizens holding passports of British National Overseas (BNO), are now citizens of a special administrative region of China. It is of particular significance to investigate how the two identities of HK people are constructed and reconstructed in the governments' PA and the co-variation between social change and discourse is of special appealing to academic researchers in sociolinguistics.

Furthermore, the association between language and identity is well established in research in the fields of language, sociology and psychology and previous studies have been carried out among varying populations against different contexts, however, most of which focused on the end-product (identity categories), rather than the construction process from a discursive perspective. In other words, their goal was often to define and categorize an individual or a group. The intention of this study therefore is to refocus so that the significance of identification as a process is brought to the fore. The study will specifically be engaged with how the construction process creates the identities of the HK people in the political discourse of PA. It is of great social significance to study the change in identity and of academic significance to uncover the processes of the discursive construction of such identities. Moreover, as HK people were British citizens before the transition and Chinese citizens after the transition, the research is to contribute some concern to the comparison of the identity construction processes pre- vs. post-transition.

Although some studies have been concerned with HK identity, most of them approached the issue from perspectives other than sociolinguistics. The only few research along this line is neither thorough nor penetrative, which is virtually based on data from wide-ranging heterogeneous genres of discourse rather than from one specific homogeneous genre. An in-depth study that focuses on one particular genre of political discourse of the two governments pre-and post-transition and that makes a comparison between the two governments should be more revealing and preferable. In such a research context, the present study is intended to delve into the issue of the discursive construction of HK identity in the governments' PA, primarily based on a theoretical framework of critical discourse analysis (henceforth CDA). CDA is selected as a major theoretical scaffolding for the present research, because it is a theory that mediates discourse and society and that it is both explanatory and interpretative due to its interdisciplinarity.

The significance of this study can thus be summed up as follows: firstly, it will uncover the relationship between language and identity, how language constructs an identity through certain discursive strategies; secondly, it will contribute to the sociolinguistic study of identity in the context of HK; thirdly, its significance further lies in its being a comparative corpus-based study of one particular genre of PA pre- vs. post-transition; lastly, it incorporates different approaches in CDA into its theoretical framework, thus generates a complete analytical framework for the study of identity construction in discourse.

## 1.2 Goals of the present research

The present research intends to gain insight into the relationship between language and identity, and how an identity is constructed through discursive strategies, and tries to draw a complete picture of the particular characteristics of the distinctive identities of Hong Kong people from both a constructive and a discursive perspective, aiming at gaining insight into the Hong Kong issue through the tools provided by discourse analysis, and more particularly critical discourse analysis. That is, this study will be based on the critical analysis of the texts of the Hong Kong governments' Policy Addresses. In contrast with the perspectives like sociology or psychology of the HK people's perception of their identity from which a series of studies have been focusing on HK identity, the present one is only concerned with the ways in which the HK governments define and present the identities of their people. Thus the present research will display the relationship between language and the identity discursively constructed in discourse. And the aim of this research is to describe how the HK governments' PA presents and constructs the distinctive identities of HK through the use of language and discursive strategies.

Thus from the above mentioned it becomes increasingly clear that there is a need to contribute to the account of sociolinguistics that this piece of research is intended to meet with its advantageous position consisting in that the scope of this research is ample and rich, and that a wealth of aspects enter into play: the need to gain an understanding of the community, plus the particular historical moment they are going through, understanding also the discursive strategies applied in the highly institutionalized genre—PA, and the process that the representative of the power, the government, is trying to construct the ideologies of the public through discourses.

Hence the piece of research seems to lie midway between linguistic and social interests since, when we come to take into account language users, social situations and culture at large, we move away from the traditional scope of linguistics and get closer to the domains of social sciences. At the same time, a social problem is dealt with from the perspectives of discourse and language use.

Moreover, it is noted that the present author engages in this task from the perspective of an outsider. Being born and brought up outside Hong Kong and an outsider to HK can prove positive since it allows a more or less neutral position in the observation and interpretation of the events. The author also hopes that the present analysis of the Hong Kong governments' Policy Address can contribute to a more conscious and critical reading of political discourse and also help to achieve a better understanding of the community of HK and its people and help the country in HK policy planning in the future.

## 1.3 Layout of the present study

The present book will be composed of the following chapters.

Chapter One is a brief introduction to our present research, including some background information of HK pre-and post-transition, the purposes and goals of this research, on which the basis for this present research is established.

Chapter Two reviews related literature of identity from which the working definition of the discursive construction of HK identity is produced, and theories in CDA which are essential to the analytical framework in the discursive construction of HK identity.

Chapter Three demonstrates the theoretical methodology in the present research based on Chapter One and Chapter Two.

Chapter Four analyses the macro-strategies in the discursive construction of HK identity in the present research data which concentrates on answering the question of what are chosen as topics in the PAs.

Chapter Five analyses the micro-strategies in the discursive construction of HK identity in the present research corpus which tries to answer how the linguistic strategies on different levels are applied in the construction of HK identity.

Chapter Six is a discussion and a comparison of the results of the macro-strategies and micro-strategies in the present corpus.

Chapter Seven tries to bring the present research to a conclusion with some major findings in this research that shed light on discursive identity construction in sociolinguistics and also a working framework for the analysis of identity construction in political discourse.

# Chapter 2 Identity and CDA

In this chapter, we will briefly review the different approaches of study on identity so as to better understand the nature of HK identity in this study and to draw out a working definition of HK identity. Then we will also trace the origin of critical discourse analysis and its present state which might help to present a clear theoretical framework from a pragmatic perspective for the present study. Finally, the perspective of the present research will be introduced with the previous review of the theories of identity and CDA, which provides a basis for working out the analytical and theoretical frameworks of the present research.

## 2.1 Literature review of identity theories

### 2.1.1 The notion of identity

The conception of identity is approached from a variety of methodological and theoretical perspectives taken from various disciplines. In this part we will briefly review the existing studies relating to identity study and try to draw some conclusions from them. This will help to achieve a better understanding of identity and also HK identity in the present research thus basing the discursive construction of HK identity in this highly institutionalized genre of PA.

#### 2.1.1.1 Identity: from a philosophical perspective

Paul Ricceur's theory (1992) distinguishes two sub-components of the equivocal term "identity": identity as sameness and identity as selfhood.

Ricceur characterizes "sameness" as a concept of relation and as a relation of relations (1992). He divides the conceptual structure of sameness into three semantic components:

*First comes numerical identity: thus, we say of two occurrences of a thing, designated by an invariable noun in ordinary language, that they do not form two different things, but "one and the same" thing. Here, identity denotes oneness: the contrary is plurality.*

*In second place we find qualitative identity, in other words, extreme resemblance: we say that x and y are wearing the same suit—that is, clothes that are similar that they are interchangeable with no noticeable difference.*

*The third component is the "uninterrupted continuity between the first and last stage in the development of that which consider to be the same individual. This criterion is predominant whenever growth and aging operate as factors of dissemblance and by implication, of numerical diversity"* (*Ricceur*, 1992).

Ricceur (1992) developed his concept of identity on the basis of the single individual, to whom he applies the concept of "selfhood" to which Martin (1995) proposed "uniqueness" "singularity" or "unmistakability" as one translation. The identity of selfhood is rooted in a model of constancy which corresponds to the temporality of human existence, and the identity of sameness is based on the constancy of a farthest-reaching invariant.

Ricceur studies not only group identity but individual identity as well, and the identity of Hong Kong People is rather of group or community or national than individual. So it can be inferred that the present study should attach importance to "sameness" rather than "selfhood" as in Ricceur's terms.

#### 2.1.1.2 Identity: from a cultural perspective

Stuart Hall describes nations not only as political formations but also as "systems of cultural representations" (1996a). A national culture is a discourse—a way of constructing meanings which influences and organizes both our actions and our conception of ourselves... National cultures construct identities by producing meanings about "the nation" with which we can identify; these are contained in the stories which are told about it, memories which connect its present with its past, and imagines which are constructed of it (Hall, 1996).

Cultural identities can be described as "identification points", as "seams which arise in the discourse of history and culture. Not anything constant, but rather a positioning" (Rathzel, 1994). According to Hall (1996), these constructed national cultural identities and national cultures are not uniform, but rather are to be thought of as a discursive sketch which represents differences between social classes, between ethnic groups or between the sexes as units "unified" by the exertion of cultural power. He further argues, in modern society, "the national cultures into which we are born are one of the principal sources of cultural identity" (Hall, 1996). He also notes that identities are "points of temporary attachment to the subject positions which discursive practices construct for us"; they are constantly in the process of change and transformation. All modern nations are "cultural hybrids" because in the course of change in the modern era, communities and organizations are integrated into new spatial and temporal relationships and brought into relation with each other.

Hall focuses more on the cultural aspect of identity and his concepts of "common stories (history)" "changeable identity" and "changing identity" shed some light on our present research.

#### 2.1.1.3 Identity: from a social perspective

Benedict Anderson (1983) describes nations—as well as all other communities that are larger than "face-to-face group"—as imagined communities and supports the view that communities are to be distinguished from one another "not by their authenticity but by the way in which they are imagined" (Anderson, 1983). Anderson continues:

*Because the members of even the smallest nations will never know most of their fellow members, meet them, or even hear of them; yet in the minds of each lives the image of their communion... The nation is imagined as limited because even the largest of them, ... has finite, if elastic, boundaries, beyond which lie other nations. …it is imagined as sovereign because the concept was born in an age in which Enlightenment and Revolution were destroying the legitimacy of the divinely-ordained, hierarchical dynastic realm.*

Anderson attaches great significance to written language in the formation of nations first for written languages make it possible for rapidly growing numbers of people to think about themselves, and to relate themselves to others and secondly because written languages lead to a fixation of language and thus of the images of the past times (Anderson, 1983). He even claims that written languages invent nationalism.

While some other sociologists employ the concept of habitus on national identities, among them are Elias (1992), Blomert, Kuzmics and Treibel (1993), Kuzmics

(1993), Paier (1996), and especially Bourdieu (1994) whose concept of habitus consists of three components—mental level, level of emotions and attitudes, level of behavioural dispositions. Bourdieu further describes the contribution of the state—or more specifically its administrators and officials—to the generation of national identities as follows:

*Through classificational systems (specially according to sex and age) inscribed in law, through bureaucratic procedures, educational structures and social rituals, the state molds mental structures and imposes common principles of vision and division... and it thereby contributes to the construction of what is commonly designated as national identity* (*Bourdieu*, 1994).

His views on identity are influential in that he claims that the state shapes those forms of perception, of categorization, of interpretation, and of memory which serve as the basis for a more or less immediate orchestration of the habitus which forms the basis for a kind of "national common sense", or national identity.

From a sociological perspective, the conclusions can be drawn that identity is discursively constructed, and habitus, language and government play important roles in the construction of national identity.

#### 2.1.1.4 Identity: from a functional-linguistic/social-semiotic perspective

Language should be studied in a social-semiotic perspective (Halliday, 1978, 1994; Halliday & Hasan, 1989) because language is integrally bound up with meaning, and all linguistic choices can be linked to the meaning they convey, but the meaning that is conveyed by language is not free-standing open to each individual to construct at will. Meaning is dependent on social context in two ways, which Halliday (1994) calls "the context of situation" and "the context of culture". Within this broad conceptualization of language as a social semiotic, Halliday proposes that language spontaneously performs three macro-functions, namely, textual, ideational and interpersonal function and he further refers in passing to the expression of "identity" as part of the interpersonal function of language.

Though Halliday describes "identity" as a sub-function of language, Roz Ivanic (1998) suggests that the three dimensions of identity correspond to the three macro-functions of language. Identity firstly consists of a person's set of values and beliefs about reality which affect the ideational meaning conveyed through language. Identity secondly consists of a person's sense of their relative status in relation to others with whom they are communicating which affects the interpersonal meaning conveyed through language. The third component of identity is a person's orientation to language use which affects their way of constructing their message.

Thus, on the one hand, identity is a sub-function of language, and on the other hand, the three macro-functions of language contribute towards the construction of identity. The way in which language constructs identity should be the focus of our present study.

#### 2.1.1.5 Identity: from a socio-political perspective

Fairclough (1989, 1992, and 1995) provides a framework for integrating a description of language with a description of its context of production in which he shows the way in which language is both shaped by and shaping its social context.

And his major contribution to the discussion of discourse and identity is that he places the construction of identity in the context of fluctuating culture and institutional values and that discourse contributes to processes of cultural change, in which the social identities associated with specific domains and institutions are redefined and reconstituted. In Fairclough's view:

*When one emphasizes construction, the identity function of language begins to assume great importance, because the ways in which societies categorize and build identities for their members is a fundamental aspect of how they work, how power relations are imposed and exercised, how societies are reproduced and changed* (*Fairclough*, 1992).

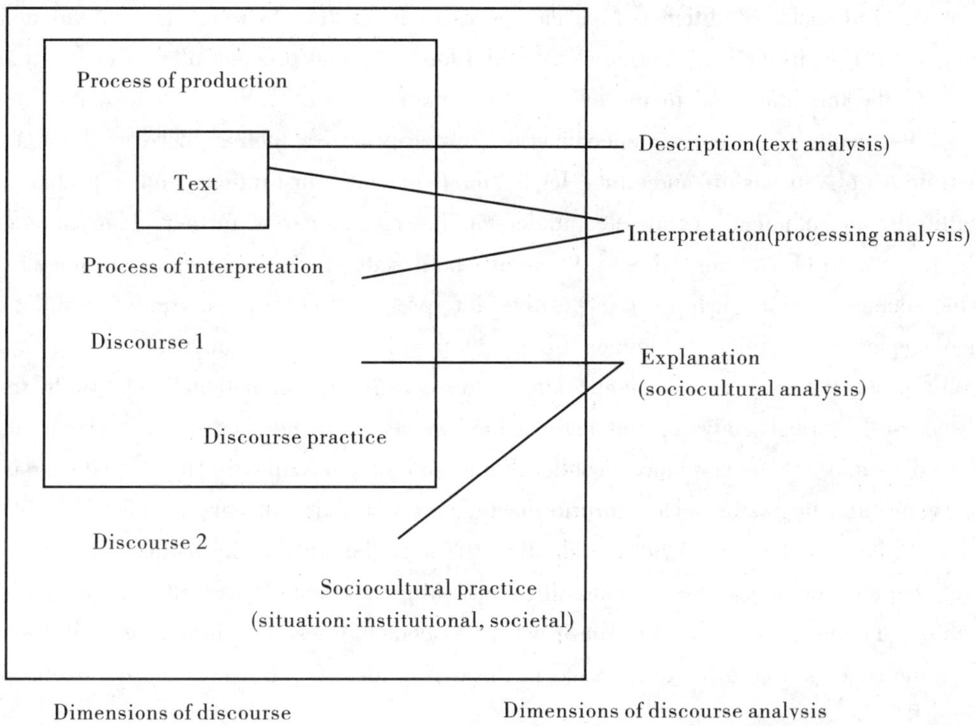


(Source for original figure: Fairclough 1995. Adapted by O'Halloran 2003)

Fairclough's framework relates social construction to social interaction, texts to other texts, discourse to identity. In conclusion, Fairclough demonstrates how language is socially constructed and probably the most powerful of all semiotic media for the social construction of reality and the construction of identity, and also identity construction in discourse covariates social-political change.

Thus in the study of identity, the factor of socio-political change cannot be avoided and in studying the institutionalized genre of the governments' Policy Address, the relation between one text and other texts should be involved.

#### 2.1.1.6 Identity: from a CDA perspective

Wodak (1999) adopts a Critical Discourse Analysis approach to the study of national identity. She holds that the national identity of individuals who perceive themselves as belonging to a national collectivity is manifested, in their social practices, one of which is discursive practice, and the respective national identity is shaped by state, political, institutional, media and everyday social practices, and the material and social conditions which emerge as their results, to which the individual is subjected. The discursive practice as a special form of social practice plays a central part both in the formation and in the expression of national identity. She tries to make clear that the concept of nation encompasses two aspects—a notion derived from the definitions of citizenship and other legal and democratic institutions and a traditional culturally and ethnically connotated understanding of nation. She further points out that the perception of a national identity contains both state-specific and cultural elements. The concept of citizenship, the positive interpretation of political and institutional achievements, language, common socio-cultural features and outstanding national-cultural achievements may all contribute to the construction of national identity. In this discourse-historical analysis, her main achievements lie in her construction of national sameness and uniqueness and also her framework of analyzing the topics, discursive strategies and linguistic devices in the discursive construction of national identity.

While after Ivanic (1998), identity refers to the idea of individuals identifying with certain social groups, communities and aligning themselves with the interests, values, beliefs and practices of these groups or communities. This definition is different in some aspects from other terms used in discussing identity, but they are not exclusive of each other.

Summarizing what has been reviewed up to this point, it is observed that the discursive construction of national identity or community identity revolves around the three temporal axes of the past, the present and the future and that origin, continuity/tradition, transformation, and anticipation are important ordering criteria. Spatial, territorial, and local dimensions (expanse, borders, nature, landscape, etc.) are likewise significant in the discursive construction of national identity. Thus national identity is on the one hand in relation to the themes of history and culture, and on the other hand in relation to the themes of "sameness" "difference" (or the "other") and "uniqueness". In order that we can analyze our body of data more systematically and completely, the present research is to base on critical discourse analysis as CDA is interdisciplinary, and at the same time draws on some theories from related perspectives in linguistics as complements.

### 2.1.2 The notion of HK identity

#### 2.1.2.1 The constructability of identity

In the past decades, interest in language and identity from disciplines such as linguistics, anthropology, psychology and sociology has experienced an unprecedented growth. Language is thought to express much more than what is signified by its words. It has been firmly established that linguistic processes and strategies play a fundamental role in the negotiation and construction of identities (De Fina, 2006). In such a context, the anti-essentialist vision of identity held by social constructionism has won wide recognition. Rather than viewing identity as something existing inside people, in the form of traits or characteristics, social constructionism regards it as the product of social encounters and relationships and, therefore, it is socially constructed in the process of negotiation in concrete and specific international occasions, entailing discursive practice (Berger & Luchman, 1967; Burr, 2003). Identity is therefore, contrasted with the traditional view of the stable unchanging personality, constantly on the move, changing from situation to situation, from encounter to encounter. In opposition to traditional beliefs, identities are understood as constructed, multiple and dynamic (Woodward, 1997; Martin, 1995; Ainsorth & Hardy, 2004).

#### 2.1.2.2 The complexity of HK identity

The acquisition of Hong Kong by Britain was the result of the infamous Opium War between 1940 and 1941. The emphasis on Hong Kong as a post for trade with China directed the British educational policy in Hong Kong in the 19th century. The policy aimed at supplying the human resource needs of the China trade and at serving the broader interests of Sino-British economic and diplomatic relations. The schools sought to produce bilingual, bicultural elites to function as middlemen between the British traders in Hong Kong and the merchants and officials of China. Great emphasis was placed on the students' learning Chinese as well as English and Confucian text was part of the curriculum.

In 1984, Britain and China had a successful diplomatic encounter in Beijing, and representatives of the two countries entered into an agreement—Sino-British Joint Declaration, that, in 1997, Britain would return the colony of HK to China. This agreement was widely hailed as a model of international co-operation, peacefully negotiated by two countries with radically different histories, cultures, ideologies and political systems (Flowerdew, 1998). In 1990, the Basic Law of HK was promulgated by the National People's Congress in Beijing which codified the constitutional framework that was to give effect to the promised "high degree of autonomy" with "HK people ruling HK" as well as to regulate central government—

SAR relations. In 1991, Bill of Rights was introduced to HK. The last Britain-appointed HK Governor, Chris Patten arrived in HK in 1992 and announced his political reform package which resulted in the deterioration of Sino-British relationship. Patten's reform package continued to be introduced into the Legislative Council (LegCo) and the first fully elected LegCo was produced in September in 1995. On the other hand, the Preparatory Committee began their work to select the first Chief Executive of the Special Administrative Region of HK. On July 1st, 1997, the People's Liberation Army troops crossing the border, HK was handed back to China, LegCo replaced by a provisional legislature and the Basic Law in force and Dong Jianhua the first Chief Executive of HKSAR. Dong resigned because of declining health in 2005 and Zeng took over him as acting chief executive and his successor.

The identity of HK people is not easily discernable. Ma & Fung (1999) describe the development of HK identity as having followed an "erratic path": it is a good example of what Martin (1995) refers to as an identity having "nothing to do with homogeneity and permanence". Although 95% of the population of HK is ethnic Chinese, these people mostly are either immigrants from the Mainland or are the children of such people (Flowerdew, 2004). Colonial policy, by minimizing contact with Mainland China, created a space for the creation of a local HK identity, which thus can be said to be determined in terms of the cultural differences between HK and the Mainland (Ma & Fung, 1999). HK people have traditionally seen themselves as sophisticated and Westernized in contrast to the less "civilized" mainlanders (Ma & Fung, 1999; Flowerdew, 2002). Even now, although the former British colony is a Special Administrative Region of China, HK people are reluctant to label themselves as "Chinese" when asked to do so in opinion surveys. They prefer to refer to themselves as "HK people" or "HK Chinese". Of course, identity is multi-faceted and in the case of the people of HK, three dimensions of identity seem to be particularly salient: ethnic identity, cultural identity and political identity which do not necessarily coincide. As to the first, no HK Chinese would be likely to deny that they are ethnically Chinese. However, politically they do not want to identify with the government of the People's Republic of China (PRC), they might say they are not "Chinese" in this political sense (Flowerdew, 2004). Then again, as suggested by Ma & Fung (1999), they might not want to be considered Chinese in the sense of sharing cultural values with mainland Chinese. This is the complicated nature of HK identity.

Several recent books and papers on HK have tried to analyze the main factors that led to the emergence of a specific HK identity. We refer to Ackbar (1997), Bhabha (1994), Baker (1983), Chen & Jackie (1997), Chen J. C. (1997), Cheng J. (1984, 1997), Faure (1996), Jacquet R. (1997), E. Kit-wai Ma (1999), Lau Siu-Kai (1982), O'Toole (1997), Scollon R. (1999), and Flowerdew (2004). These factors include the territory's prolonged separation from China, the coming to adulthood of a generation born in the colony, the benefits of the economic boom, and the Government's social reforms in the 1970s and after, the control of the PRC Government over the HKSAR Government and the economic boom in Mainland China as well.

Even though ethnic Chinese make up 95% of the population, English was the only official language until 1974. While Cantonese has always been the language of the home, English still remains essential for education, business, the government, and the law. Whereas in the past English might have been perceived as the colonial language, English has now become the international language of upward and outward mobility, enabling HK people to enter university, to take on positions in the HK international business world, or to go overseas to study or to emigrate.

However complex HK identities are, it is definite and explicit that before the 1997 Transition, HK people were British citizens nominally according to the previous Common Law of HK because they held the passports of British National Overseas issued by the British Government, and that after transition, HK people are Chinese citizens as HK is a region of China and it accords with the Basic Law.

#### 2.1.2.3 The co-variation of the discursive identity construction with the transition

The basic premise on which the present research is based is the interdependency between language and social reality. As already introduced, the research intends to show how HK identity is represented and constructed based on linguistic evidences.

Language use is shaped socially and the variation in language use is systematic and that what makes it systematic is its correlation with social variables: language varies according to the nature of the relation between participants in interaction, the type of social event, the social goals people are pursuing, and so forth.

On the one hand, discourse is shaped and constrained by social structure in the widest sense and at all levels; on the other hand, discourse is socially constitutive and contributes to the constitution of all those dimensions of social structure which directly or indirectly shape or constrain it: its own norms and conventions as well as the relations, identities and institutions which lie behind them. We can distinguish three aspects of the constructive effects of discourse. Discourse contributes first of all to the construction of what are variously referred to as "social identities" and "subject positions" for social "subjects" and types of "self". Secondly, discourse helps construct social relationships between people. And lastly, discourse contributes to the construction of systems of knowledge and belief. Thus, discourse, identities and social practice in time-space form a mutually constituting set implicated in the cultural politics of identity and the constitution of humanity as a form of life. It is the very plasticity of identity that marks its cultural and political significance, for the shifting and changing character of identities chronicles the way that people think about themselves and others at a given time and space.

Socio-political change has a great impact on discourse and identity construction in the highly institutionalized genre of HK governments' Policy Address. Therefore, the transition of Hong Kong sovereignty on July 1st, 1997 "has been complex, subtle and profound... this is because the real transition is about identity and not sovereignty" (Yeung, 1998; Chan, 2002). Therefore, the fact is evident that the British Colonial Hong Kong Government tried to construct a Hong Kong identity relating to Britain while the HKSAR Government tries to construct a Chinese Hong Kong identity in such a highly institutionalized genre as Policy Address.

The present research is to study and compare the two identities discursively constructed in the HK governments' Policy Addresses pre- and post-transition and to find out the constructive strategies employed in such a genre.

#### 2.1.2.4 HK identity: relationship with Mainland China

In the specific discipline of linguistics, identity is also attracting increasing attention. Social linguistic investigations such as those made by Labov's (1963) and Milroy's (1980) have proved that language is used as a means of expressing social identity when different ethic groups use language to align with certain social groups and to disassociate from others. Systemic Functional Linguistics (SFL) proposes that language performs simultaneously three meanings, or "metafunctions" (e.g., Halliday, 1994; Halliday & Mathiessen, 1999). Among the three meanings, namely ideational meaning, textual meaning and interpersonal meaning, interpersonal meaning refers to the use of language to negotiate social relations—to express the "self" and influence others. Hence, it can be concluded that identity is a concept of "self" in relation to its contrary of "other" and can be defined in relations.

Communication is what makes relationships possible and the specificity of the human species is that the privileged medium of communication, unknown to other species, is language (Martin, 1995). Martin suggests that it is language that makes it possible for members of a community to enter into relation with one another and it is precisely through the use of language that differences and values of a collectivity are expressed. Hence, language lies at the heart of the notion and expression of identity. Discourse becomes an "instrument for constructing an 'imagined community'" (Martin, 1995). Following Wodak, et al. (1999), identity is the product of discourse. Fairclough (1995) also considers that the questions of identity and questions of relations are inseparable in practice: how an identity is constructed is in part a question of how one relates to another.

In order to have a thorough and comprehensive study of the political discourse of the governments' Policy Address, the represent research, according to Ivanic's definition of identity, takes into consideration the social, political, cultural and discoursal factors of the society of HK and the PA of the two governments in HK. In this research, the study of HK identity in the governments' PA refers to the study whether or not the ideas demonstrated in HK governments' PA identify with the social groups, communities in mainland China and align HK and HK people with the interests, values, beliefs and practices of Mainland China. In other words, the HK identity discursively constructed in the two HK governments' PA are defined in the relationship to Mainland China.

Thus, the working definition of the discursively constructed HK identity in the present study should take the following aspects into consideration:

①HK identity is discursively, by means of language, produced, represented, and constructed;

②HK identity can be regarded as a complex of common ideas, values, concepts, attitudes, plans, history, etc. In other words, the construction of identities is to construct the in-group commonness, sameness, which goes hand in hand with the construction of out-group difference and uniqueness (Hall, 1994, 1996; Martin, 1995);

③HK identity revolves around the three temporal axes of past, present and future;

④Identities can be expressed in the kind of relations aligning or alienating oneself with another party, which, in this research, is reflected in HK's relations with

Mainland China;

⑤There is no such thing as the one and only national identity in an essentializing sense, but rather that different identities are discursively constructed according to contexts, that is according to the social field, the situational setting of the discursive act and the topic being discussed. In other words, identities are not completely consistent, stable and immutable and they co-vary with socio-political changes like the 1997 HK transition of its sovereignty.

### 2.1.3 Studies on Hong Kong identity

A series of studies on HK identity have been focusing on the HK people's perception of their identity with quite contradictory outcomes. A review of such research may shed light on our present study as only discourse that accords with people's cognitive framework can be accepted and help constitute reality (You & Chen, 2010), and in addition, no government can construct an identity of its people in opposition to its people's attitude, expectation and perception.

#### 2.1.3.1 Lau Siu-kai's study

Lau (1997) conducted a series of questionnaire surveys on the problem of the identity of HK people and when asked about their identities whether they identified themselves as "Hongkongese" "Chinese" "both", or "neither", the vast majority of the respondents had no difficulty choosing with Hongkongese or Chinese as their primary identity and the Hongkongese identity was adopted by more respondents than the Chinese identity. The findings are shown below.

**Table 1 Identities of the HK Chinese**

| | Hongkongese (%) | Chinese (%) | Both (%) | Neither (%) | Don't know (%) |
|---|---|---|---|---|---|
| 1985 | 59.5 | 36.2 | | | 4.3 |
| 1988 | 63.6 | 28.8 | | 2.0 | 5.6 |
| 1990 | 57.2 | 26.4 | 12.1 | 1.0 | 3.4 |
| 1991 | 56.6 | 25.4 | 14.2 | 1.2 | 2.4 |
| 1992 | 49.3 | 27.0 | 21.1 | 0.7 | 1.9 |
| 1993 | 53.3 | 32.7 | 10.1 | 1.6 | 2.4 |
| 1994 | 56.5 | 24.2 | 16.0 | 0.5 | 2.8 |
| 1995 | 50.2 | 30.9 | 15.4 | 1.2 | 2.8 |

Lau further points out that the survey findings showed the socio-demographic differences between the Hongkongese and Chinese—females are more likely to identify themselves as Hongkongese than males, the more educated people were also more inclined to call themselves Hongkongese, respondents who were born in HK were more likely to see themselves as Hongkongese, those who had a stronger sense of belonging to HK were more prepared to leave this community before 1997 because they were more worried about HK's future.

As a matter of fact, instead of two totally separate or mutually exclusive identities, the identities of Hongkongese and Chinese overlapped considerably as "Chineseness" in the ethnic sense and in the historical-cultural sense was an integral component in both the Hongkongese and the Chinese identities and was the basis for all of them to see themselves as Chinese. For example, in traditional China, the country or the group was accorded a status and importance much superior to the individual. Lau's 1993 survey showed that the long period of Westernization and limited governance in HK had failed to drastically transform the HK Chinese' conception of the proper relationship between the individual and the country in the abstract. Furthermore, despite their different identities, both the Hongkongese and Chinese were proud of the same set of things about Hong Kong and China—mostly about economic development and things related to it.

In his survey, Lau found that the most salient differences between the Hongkongese and the Chinese were their attitudes towards the PRC, the mainland Chinese and the Chinese central government. The greater mistrust of China on the part of the Hongkongese were in line with their greater support for Britain and the fact that they had a more favorable image of colonial rule than the Chinese and were more inclined to demand that Britain take a strong approach to China. According to Lau, HK Chinese, particularly those with the Hongkongese identity, were jolted by the June Fourth Incident in such a way that they were fully aware of their common political fate, which was perceived to be uncertain and miserable. The year 1989 can be considered as a milestone in the formation of the local identity among the HK people. Moreover, in this study, it is evident that still a small percentage of people did not know or were not certain of their identity, which further illustrates that the identity of HK people is complicated and problematic and needs further research.

#### 2.1.3.2 The Public Opinion Programmes conducted by Hong Kong University and Hong Kong Chinese University

HK University conducted a survey anniversarily to examine HK people's attitude towards their particular identity. The poll, entitled "People's Ethnic Identity Before and After the Handover", has been carried out every June since 1997. People of age 18 or above were interviewed and asked whether they are proud of formally becoming a national citizen of China after the 1997 Handover. The 1997 results show that advocates for "Yes" and "No" were close to equal, with 46.6% and 45.7% respectively. However, there has been significant change in the results since 1998, which has remained fairly steady since. In June 1998, 31.6% of the 555 respondents said "Yes", 65.7% answered "No", and the remainder said "Don't know/Hard to say". In a poll conducted in June 2001, 35.4% of the 1 074 respondents said "Yes", 59.9% said "No", and the rest "Don't know/Hard to say". These results add to the general picture that Hong Kong people's identification with the Mainland is still rather shallow. According to a poll conducted by the Chinese University's Hong Kong's Institute of Asia-Pacific Studies, 75.9% of the 1 002 respondents wanted to elect the Chief Executive through universal suffrage. When asked how long they think it would take for universal suffrage to be realised in Hong Kong, 38% said not until 10 years or more, 21% said 5 ~ 10 years, and 8% said never (Abraham, 2002; Hong Kong Economic Journal, 2002). In conclusion, Hong Kong people are maintaining their identity as distinct from that of the Mainland.

The above study and survey further show that HK identity is a complex issue on which HK people themselves cannot come to agreement and there is still confusion in HK identity which leads to room for further research. The HK people's perception of their identity may have an effect on its government and the policy makers, but it is not of concern in this research. The key issue here focuses on how the HK governments define the identity of its people in their Policy Address, which becomes the concern of this research.

#### 2.1.3.3 A summary of identity studies

In this part, we review identity research in different perspectives from different disciplines and draw a working definition for the discursively constructed identity, particularly HK identity. Furthermore, some research on HK identity from approaches other than CDA are reviewed in order to show the complexity of this HK identity. It is also our aim here to declare that HK people's attitude toward their identity is not a focus of this research, but the British Colonial HK Government, and the HKSAR Government as a partly elected government, cannot go completely against its people's opinions and attitudes in their PAs.

## 2.2 Critical Discourse Analysis

### 2.2.1 The understanding of CDA

The terms Critical Linguistics or Critical Discourse Analysis which are often used interchangeably, are considered to be a step further than Discourse Analysis (DA). Discourse analysis is the examination of language use by members of a speech community. It emerged in the 1960's from a variety of other disciplines and approaches. Zelling Harris, with his analysis of an advert text in his early Discourse Analysis (1952) is considered as the starting point of discourse studies (Renkema, 2004).

The notion of discourse is essentially difficult to define (Pennycook, 1994; Widdowson 1995; van Dijk, 1997a; Wodak, 1996), because it "has perhaps the widest range of possible significations of any term in literary and cultural theory, and yet it is often the term within theoretical texts which is least defined" (Mills, 1997). According to Jaworski and Coupland's (1999), "discourse falls squarely within the interests not only of linguists, literary critics, recital theorists and communication scientists, but also of geographers, philosophers, political scientists, sociologists, anthropologists, social psychologists, and many others". Van Dijk (1997a) defines discourse as a communicative event, that is, as language use in context and the concept of discourse should involve three dimensions: form, meaning, and action.

DA now involves looking at both language form and language function and includes the study of both spoken interaction and written texts. It identifies linguistic features that characterize different genres as well as social and cultural factors that aid in our interpretation and understanding of different texts and types of talk. A discourse analysis of written texts might include a study of topic development and cohesion across the sentences, while an analysis of spoken language might focus on these aspects plus turn-taking practices, opening and closing sequences of social encounters, or narrative structure.

The study of discourse has developed in a variety of disciplines—sociolinguistics, anthropology, sociology, and social psychology (Beaugrande, 1997). Thus discourse analysis takes different theoretical perspectives and analytic approaches: speech act theory, interactional sociolinguistics, ethnography of communication, pragmatics, conversation analysis, and variation analysis (Schiffrin, 1994).

Van Dijk (2003) summarizes the work of discourse in general as follows:

*Compared to the primitive "text grammars" of the early* 1970*s, contemporary formal work on discourse structures is of course much more sophisticated. And compared to the simplistic cognitive, social and interactional models of text and talk of* 20 *years ago, new work on text processing, socio-political discourse studies and conversational analysis also has much advanced.*

As Brown and Yule (1983) suggest, in the interpretation of discourse analysts have to take account of the context in which a piece of discourse occurs, since it will be that contextual information that will enable the analyst to arrive at the appropriate interpretation (and also Titscher, et al., 1998; Wodak, et al., 1990). It is exactly this context specificity which distinguishes DA from the ethnomethodological conversation analysis, which analyses communication processes out of context (Wodak, et al., 1990). Context usually has a variety of dimensions: sociological, political, institutional, psychological, historical etc. Broadly speaking, three levels of context may be distinguished (Wodak, 1998). On the lowest level, this is the so-called co-text, which is the immediate, language-internal, or, in linguistic terms, syn-semantic surrounding of a particular instance of language use. On a higher level, an utterance is made in a specific, language-external setting. Setting in this understanding comprises the characteristics of the institutional setting which are non-linguistic—it not only makes a difference whether one speaks in parliament or at home, but also the characteristics of the discourse participants, such as the nationality and sex of the speaker. And, of particular importance in an approach named "discourse-historical" is of course the historical setting within which texts are being produced. Obviously, concentration on one aspect or another of context will very much depend on the dimension from which the analyst approaches discourse analysis. The third level of context does not fit into the high and low categorization which is a concept much more prominent and significant in CDA. It is the intertextual references of a specific utterance. Here one looks for traces of other texts in the text under examination. References to other texts may take a variety of forms, from explicit quotes to subtle allusions.

However, the actual research is not organised as a two-step of context analysis followed by discourse analysis. Rather, contexts and discourse are looked at as interconnected and it is the parallel and blended analysis of both that makes for a discourse analysis.

The kind of discourse analysis which comprises the analysis of broad aspects of the societal context in which discourse is produced is first termed social discourse analysis by van Dijk (1997a) and has come to be critical discourse analysis. According to its practitioners, CDA is considered a step further than DA because it is based on the view that language is a central element in social life and hence it analyses social life in its discursive aspect. CDA attempts to disclose the ways societal structures and processes are encoded in the discourse practices. Understanding discourse as a socio-semiotic process (M. A. K. Halliday, 1978), exponents of CDA assume that public discourse not only reflects patterns of (asymmetrical) societal organization (i. e., hierarchy, power, hegemony), but also helps construct, re-enforce and reproduce them. By raising the public awareness of the encoded ideologies (systems of values and sets of beliefs) which pervade the strategies of influence, manipulation, persuasion employed by those in power (e. g., structures of politics, popular media and consumer industry) these practices can not only be disclosed ("demystified"), but also altered. This special concern of the critical analysts' is what distinguishes CDA from DA. In brief, the work of CDA is mainly aimed at providing social criticism based on linguistic evidence. This implies a constant shunting back and forth between linguistic categories of text analysis and concepts form social cultural theories. Hence, DA can be said to be an originally descriptive approach, while CDA add critical and ideological goals to the analysis of text and talk (Johnstone, 2002). In Billig's (2003) words, "critical discourse analysis implies that it is insufficient merely to study discourse as linguists have traditionally done. Linguistic analysis needs to be augmented by critical social analysis". Thus, CDA can be conceived as a step further in discourse analysis as it is critical of the present social order, of other non-critical paradigm and especially of dominant positions (Billig, 2003).

CDA is a rapidly developing area of language study. It regards discourse as "a form as social practice" (Fairclough & Wodak, 1997), and takes consideration of the context of language use to be crucial to discourse (Wodak, 2001). It takes particular interest in the relation between language and power. CDA may be described as neo-Marxist; claiming that cultural and economic dimensions are significant in the creation and maintenance of power relations. The key figures in this area include Fairclough (1992a, b, c, 1993, 1995a, b, 1996, 1998, 2000, 2001, 2003), van Dijk (1993, 1997, 1998a, b, 1999, 2001), Gee (1999, 2005), van Leeuwen (1993, 1995, 1996), Wodak (1996, 2000, 2001) and Scollon (2001). It is generally agreed that CDA cannot be classified as a single method but is rather viewed as an approach, which consists of different perspectives and different methods for studying the relationship between the use of language and social context.

There have been many attempts to systematize CDA. The most notable work has been conducted by Fairclough (1992a, 1995a, 1998, 2000, 2001, 2003), Chouliaraki & Fairclough (1999), van Dijk (1993, 1997, 2001), Wodak (1996, 2001), Scollon (1998, 1999, 2001, 2004), Gee (1999, 2005) and van Leeuwen (1993, 1995, 1996). Though they vary considerably in technical specification, they share a common strategy. In Luke's words:

*CDA involves a principled and transparent shunting back and forth between the microanalysis of texts using varied tools of linguistics, semiotic, and literary analysis and the macroanalysis of social formations, institutions, and power relations that these texts index and construct* (*Luke*, 2002).

Consequently, attempts to systematize CDA draw from theories and models of text analysis on one hand, and from contemporary political and sociocultural theories on the other. Some approaches, such as Fairclough (1992a, 2001) and Wodak (1996), rely much on a linguistic analysis of texts, especially Halliday's (1985, 1994, 2004) systemic functional linguistics (SFL), beginning with systematic analysis of lexical resources, moving through an analysis of syntactic functions to the analysis of genre and text metafunction. In contrast with approaches of Fairclough and Wodak, van Dijk (1997) and Gee (1999, 2005) both develop toolkits that are less oriented to lexicosyntactic features of texts and more focused on cultural and social resources and contexts. Van Dijk's (1997) approach is based on four categories: action, context, power and ideology, while Gee's (1999, 2005) methodological heuristics is based on six categories: semiotic building, world building, activity building, identity and relationship building, political building, connection building.

Luke (2002) argues that "a linguistic and text analytic metalanguage, no matter how comprehensive, cannot 'do' CDA in and of itself. It requires the overlay of a social theoretic discourse for explaining and explicating the social contexts, concomitants, contingencies and consequences of any given text or discourse." Pennycook (2001) also claims that what texts "do" in the world cannot be explained solely through text analysis or text analytic language.

With regard to macro analyses, CDA attempts to move beyond text analysis to the critical analysis of the visible practices of text interpretation and use. Fairclough (1992a), Gee (1999, 2005), and Chouliaraki & Fairclough (1999) engage with a range of major social theories as they do this. This study is based largely on the linguistic stream of a CDA drawing on the work of Fairclough, van Dijk and Wodak as the basis for its analytical framework.

### 2.2.2 The development of CDA

In the late 1970s, Critical Linguistics (CL) was developed by a group of linguists and literary theorists at the University of East Anglia (Fowler, et al., 1979; Kress & Hodge, 1979). Their approach was based on Halliday's Systemic Functional Linguistics (SFL). CL practitioners such as Trew (1979) aimed at "isolating ideology in discourse" and showed "how ideology and ideological processes are manifested as systems of linguistic characteristics and processes". This aim was pursued by developing CL's analytical tools (Fowler, et al., 1979; Fowler, 1991) based on SFL.

Following Halliday, these CL practitioners view language in use as simultaneously performing three functions: ideational, interpersonal, and textual functions. According to Fowler (1991). and Fairclough (1995b), whereas the ideational function refers to the experience of the speakers of the world and its phenomena; the interpersonal function embodies the insertion of speakers' own attitudes and evaluations about the phenomena in question, and establishes a relationship between speakers and listeners. Instrumental to these two functions is the textual function. It is through the textual function of language that speakers are able to produce texts that are understood by listeners. It is an enabling function connecting discourse to the co-text and con-text in which it occurs.

Halliday's view of language as a "social act" is central to many of CDA's practitioners (Chouliaraki & Fairclough, 1999; Fairclough, 1989, 1992, 1993, 1995b, 1995a; Fowler, et al., 1979; Fowler, 1991; Hodge & Kress, 1979). According to Fowler, et al. (1979), CL, like sociolinguistics, asserts that, "there are strong and pervasive connections between linguistic structure and social structure". However, whereas in sociolinguistics "the concepts 'language' and 'society' are divided... so that one is forced to talk of 'links between the two'", for CL "language is an integral part of social process" (Fowler, et al., 1979).

Another central assumption of CDA and SFL is that speakers make choices regarding vocabulary and grammar, and that these choices are consciously or unconsciously "principled and systematic" (Fowler, et al., 1979). Thus choices are ideologically based. According to Fowler, et al. (1979), the "relation between form and content is not arbitrary or conventional, but... form signifies content". In sum, language is a social act and it is ideologically driven.

Over the years CL and what is more frequently referred to as CDA (Chouliaraki & Fairclough, 1999; van Dijk, 1998a) has been further developed and broadened. Recent work has raised some concerns with the earlier work in CL. Among the concerns was, first, taking into consideration the role of audiences and their interpretations of discourse possibly different from that of the discourse analyst. The second concern has called for broadening the scope of analysis beyond the textual, extending it to the intertextual analysis.

Fairclough (1995b) has raised both issues. He claims that the earliest work in CDA did not adequately focus on the "interpretive practices of audiences". In other words, he claims that CDA has, for the most part, assumed that the audiences interpret texts the same way the analysts do. In a similar vein, commenting on Fowler (1991), Boyd-Barrett (1994) asserts that there is "a tendency towards the classic fallacy of attributing particular 'readings' to readers, or media 'effects', solely on the basis of textual analysis".

The other issue put forward by Fairclough (1995b) is that while earlier contributions in CL were very thorough in their grammatical and lexical analysis they were less attentive to the intertextual analysis of texts: "the linguistic analysis is very much focused upon clauses, with little attention to higher-level organization properties of whole texts." Despite raising these issues with regards to earlier works in CL, Fairclough (1995b) inserts that "mention of these limitations is not meant to minimize the achievement of critical linguistics—they largely reflect shifts of focus and developments of theory in the past twenty years or so". The "shifts of focus and developments of theory" which Fairclough (1995b) talks about, however, have not resulted in the creation of a single theoretical framework. What is known today as CDA, according to Bell & Garret (1998), "is best viewed as a shared perspective encompassing a range of approaches rather than as just one school". Also, van Dijk (1998a) tells us that CDA "is not a specific direction of research", hence "it does not have a unitary theoretical framework". But, van Dijk (1998a) asserts, "given the common perspective and the general aims of CDA, we may also find overall conceptual and theoretical frameworks that are closely related".

### 2.2.3 General principles in CDA

Though CDA does not have a unitary theoretical framework, it is based on some general principles. What follows is a summary of the most widely cited principles of Fairclough & Wodak's (1997) which gives further support of CDA being the starting point of the present research.

(1) CDA addresses social problems.

CDA is the analysis of linguistic and semiotic aspects of social processes and problems. The focus is not upon language or the use of language in and for themselves, but upon the partially linguistic character of social and cultural processes and structures. Furthermore, CDA is by its nature interdisciplinary, combining diverse disciplinary perspectives in its own analyses, and being used to complement more standard forms of social and cultural analysis. Particularly it achieves a dominant position in the field of political discourse. As the present research is to address the social problem of HK identity in the political discourse of the governments' Policy Addresses, CDA helps to develop a critical awareness of the discursive strategies applied in the construction of national/community identity.

(2) Power relations are discursive.

CDA highlights the substantively linguistic and discursive nature of social relations of power in contemporary societies. This is partly a matter of how power relations are exercised and negotiated in discourse and how power is realized in linguistic devices. In the research of the discursive construction of identity in the governments' Policy Addresses, it is to reveal the influence the transition of the power and sovereignty has exerted on the social problem of identity and linguistic devices. In addition to the question of power in discourse, there is the question of power over discourse (Fairclough, 1989) . Be the Governor of HK or the Executive of the HKSAR the person with the supreme responsibility for this area, the way he exercised his power over the Policy Addresses is most significant. CDA is fruitful to look at both "power in discourse" and "power over discourse" —both the exercise of power in specific discursive events and the long term shaping of discursive practices are the focuses of it.

(3) Discourse constitutes society and culture.

We can only make sense of the salience of discourse in contemporary social processes and power relations by recognizing that discourse constitutes society and culture, as well as being constituted by them. Their relationship is a dialectical one. This entails that every instance of language use makes its own small contribution to reproducing and/or transforming society and culture. The three broad domains of social life that may be discursively constituted are representations, relations and identities for short: representations of the world, social relations between people, and people's social and personal identities (Fairclough, 1992a) . These three domains harmonizes with a multifunctional theory of language and text in systemic functional linguistics (Halliday, 1994) . According to this theory, a text simultaneously functions "ideationally" in representing reality, and "interpersonally" in constructing social relations and identities, as well as "textually" in making the parts of a text into a coherent whole.

(4) Discourse does ideological work.

Ideologies are particular ways of representing and constructing society which reproduce unequal relations of power, relations of domination and exploitation. The theory of ideology is now extended to include relations of domination based upon gender and ethnicity. Ideology is not just a matter of representations of social reality, for constructions of identity which are linked to power are key ideological processes too. It is useful to think of ideology as a process which articulates together particular representations of reality, and particular constructions of identity, especially of the collective identities of groups and communities. In this case, the ideological work that is being researched is representations of different identities of the same group of people and the strategies for the construction of "the people".

(5) Discourse is historical.

Discourse is not produced without context and cannot be understood without taking the context into consideration (Duranti & Goodwin, 1992; Wodak, et al., 1990, 1994). Utterances are only meaningful if we consider their use in a specific situation, if we understand the underlying conventions and rules, if we recognize the embedding in a certain culture and ideology, and most importantly, if we know what the discourse relates to the past. Discourses are always connected to other discourses which were produced earlier, as well as those which are produced synchronically and subsequently. As our present study is to uncover the change of identity of the same community, a discourse-historical approach has to be employed with the socio-cultural aspects as the context.

(6) The link between text and society Is mediated.

CDA is much more about making connections between social and cultural structures and processes on the one hand, and properties of text on the other. But these connections are rather complex, and are best seen as indirect or "mediated" rather than direct. Changes of discourse are realized in features of language, making an indirect, mediated link between socio-cultural processes and linguistic properties of texts. Thus CDA is appropriately useful in penetrating the discursive construction of identities in the governments' Policy Addresses with the social change—the transition as the background.

(7) Discourse analysis is interpretative and explanatory.

Discourse can be interpreted in very different ways, and only CDA may deconstruct the text and show the different implications of different meanings for social action when we deal with historical and synchronic intertextuality, the hybridization of genres and the opaqueness of certain elements and units, because CDA implies a systematic methodology and a thorough investigation of the context and thus narrows down the whole range of possible interpretations. The heterogeneity and vagueness of the text condenses contradictions which only become apparent through careful analysis. When deconstructed and embedded in its social conditions, the text is linked to ideologies and power relationships, as is the point where CDA differs from an uncritical reading. But it has to be emphasized that interpretations and explanations are never finished and exhaustive; they are dynamic and open to new contexts.

(8) Discourse is a form of social action.

The principle of CDA is to uncover opaqueness and power relationships. CDA is a socially committed scientific paradigm. There exists a lot examples of important applications of CDA as in education (van Dijk, 1993a), politics (Fairclough, 1992c), court (Gruber & Wodak, 1992), etc. Moreover, CDA has had much success in changing discourse and power patterns in institutions. The critical analysis of doctor-patient communication patterns (Lalouschek, et al., 1990; West, 1990) led to guidelines for different behaviour patterns, which were and are taught in seminars for doctors. The same is true for other institutions, for bureaucracies, legal institutions and schools (Funnarsson, 1989; Danet, 1984; Pfeiffer, et al., 1987).

Based on the above eight principles of CDA, and as far as the research goal and research questions of the present study are concerned, CDA is the most appropriate approach in looking into such social problems of the identity of Hong Kong people, which in turn pivots that our present research should be done within the framework of CDA.

### 2.2.4 Critiques of CDA

Criticism of CDA comes from scholars in the area of conversation analysis (CA) and other fields of text analysis. The antecedent to the debate between CDA and CA is a paper written by Schegloff, titled "Whose text? Whose context?" (Schegloff, 1997) and a reaction by Wetherell (1998) to this paper. Schegloff argues that CDA is often short on detailed, systematic analysis of text or talk, for instance as it is carried out in conversation analysis. Wetherell (1998) replies that CA and CDA are not in conflict even though they are in some way incompatible research areas, and while CDA is interested in social problems, CA is concerned with structure problems in the organization of conversation.

Along with the general debate about CDA, a specific discussion has developed between Norman Fairclough (1996) and Henry Widdowson (1995, 1998) over CDA. Widdowson claims that the term "discourse" as it is used in CDA is as vague as it is fashionable: "discourse is something everybody is talking about but without knowing with any certainty just what it is: in vogue and vague" (Widdowson, 1995). Widdowson also criticizes the lack of a clear demarcation between text and discourse. Furthermore, he argues that CDA is an ideological interpretation and therefore not an analysis. The term critical discourse analysis is a contradiction in terms, he says. Widdowson believes that "CDA is, in a dual sense, a biased interpretation: in the first place it is prejudiced on the basis of some ideological commitment, and then it selects for analysis such texts as will support the preferred interpretation" (Widdowson, 1995). Analysis, he argues, ought to mean the examination of several interpretations and, in the case of CDA, this is not possible because of prior judgments. Fairclough (1996), in reply to this criticism, draws attention to the open-endedness of results required in CDA. He also points out that CDA, unlike most other approaches, is always explicit about its own position and commitment.

Toolan (1997, 2002) and Stubbs (1997) also make some criticisms of CDA, arguing for a strengthening of the theorization of CDA. Toolan (1997) argues that first, some theoretical distinctions in CDA, such as the difference between description and interpretative explanation need to be further clarified. Second, CDA needs to be more critical and more demanding of the text linguistics it uses. Third, in doing CDA thorough and strong evidence should be collected for the arguments made while simple presentation of the analytical findings should be pursued.

After pointing out several fundamental criticisms of CDA, such as CDA's methods of data collection and text analysis, Stubbs (1997) puts forward eleven "essential questions" in an effort to "rescue" CDA from the circularity of theory. In Stubbs' view, CDA provides no systematic comparisons between texts and norms in the language, and "language and thought can only be related if one has data and theory pertinent to both: otherwise the theory is circular" (Stubbs, 1997). By this, he means that if language use influences a person's view of reality, there must be non-linguistic evidence of a pattern of beliefs and behaviour to support this claim. If we have no independent evidence for what we claim, but infer beliefs from language use, then the theory is circular.

Although there are criticisms of CDA, these do not distract from the value of work in the area of CDA. Many theorists share strong political starting points for doing CDA, with their major focus on revealing hidden values, beliefs and bias of texts, and studying power relationship behind texts. Many of them, however, establish operationalised research frameworks for exploring relationships between language use and social context. The work of Fairclough, Wodak and van Leeuwen especially have helped to operationalise the principles of CDA and are of value to answering the research questions of the present study. In this regard, the words of van Dijk in his 2001 article "Multidisciplinary CDA: a plea for diversity" makes an important contribution. He writes,

*In my many years of experience as editor of several international journals, I have found that contributions that imitate and follow some great master are seldom original. Without being eclectic, good scholarship, and especially good CDA, should integrate the best work of many people, famous or not, from different disciplines, countries, cultures and directions of research. In other words, CDA should be essentially diverse and multidisciplinary.* (*van Dijk*, 2001).

CDA, then, is a comprehensive approach to studying the relationship between language use and its social context. Van Dijk's words cast insights on the present study and its research framework.

### 2.2.5 Van Dijk's (1997) and Wodak's (1999) different approaches to CDA

Because of its own nature and evolution, CDA does not have a homogeneous approach. It comprises a wide range of methods and theoretical frameworks depending on the analyst's own interests and tendencies (Sheyholislami, 2001; Wodak, et al., 1999; Meyer, 2001). Basically, CDA practitioners need to bring together linguistic and sociological categories in their analyses, through a synthesis of the different conceptual tools that best suit the research questions they address. They are, thus, an heterogeneous group who nonetheless share some analytical principles and a concern with certain issues manifested through discourse (Blommaert, 2005). Threadgold (2003) claims that the heterogeneity of methods is characteristic of this field. A basic reason is that "complex new problems, such as identity research, racism research, and so on, require more than the expertise of an individual discipline" (Weiss & Wodak, 2003). This leads to a further characteristic of CDA, its interdisciplinarity (Weiss & Wodak, 2003). Interdisciplinary work implies that once the topic of research has been identified, the critical discourse analyst has to look for methodologies, theoretical frameworks and categories that suit it. Hence, the topics that are most frequently addressed by critical discourse analysts include: racism (van Dijk, 1986; Reisigl & Wodak, 2001; Var Der Valk, 2003), gender and sexism (Caldas-Coulthard, 1999; Marchin & Thornborrow, 2003), war and political strategies (Fairclough, 2000; Chouliaraki, 2004; Butt et al., 2004), and language domination and inequalities in institutional settings (Fairclough, 1995a: 130; Wodak, et al., 1999; Hobbs, 2003). Indeed van Dijk (2001) has emphasized the need for CDA to be diverse, broad and multidisciplinary in order to properly fulfill its goals.

Therefore, the work of the salient critical discourse analysts illustrates the variety of approaches that operate within the common perspective CDA: Norman Fairclough is mainly concerned with the application of CDA to social research and practice, while van Dijk's most recent work concentrates on cognitive aspects. Gunter Kress and Theo van Leeuwen have developed a multimodal analysis (van Leeuwen, 2004). Ruth Wodak has introduced a focus on a discourse-historical approach (Wodak, 2001a), and Ron Scollon (2001) has differentiated and termed his approach Mediated Discourse Analysis on the grounds that he pays special attention to social action and actors, and discourse is just one among the many factors that have to be analysed.

(1) Van Dijk's (1997) socio-cognitive approach.

The main representative of this approach in Teun van Dijk, most of whose critical work focuses on the (re)production of ethnic prejudices and racism in discourse and communication. In his studies about minorities (van Dijk, 1984, 1987), he aimed at reconstructing ethnic attitudes and ideologies from everyday conversation by analyzing the frequent topics which are hierarchies of "personal mental models of ethnic events and as well as of ethnic attitudes". Van Dijk also turns to more general questions of abuse of power and the reproduction of inequality through ideologies. In his view, which integrates elements form his studies on cognition, those who control most dimensions of discourse (preparation, setting, participants, topics, style, rhetoric, interaction, etc.) have the most power. He argues that no direct relation can or should be constructed between discourse structures and social structures, but that they are always mediated by the interface of personal and social cognition. Cognition, according to van Dijk, is the missing link of many studies in CDA, which fail to show how societal structures influence discourse structures and precisely how societal structures are in turn enacted, instituted, legitimated, confirmed or challenged by discourse. Theoretically, it is shown that in order to be able to relate power and discourse in an explicit way, we need the cognitive interface of models, knowledge, attitudes and ideologies and other social representations of the social mind, which also relate the individual and the social, and the micro- and the macro-levels of social structure. It is more recently that van Dijk (2001, 2003, 2005) has taken up a more detailed study of the role of cognition in discourse which is a new approach to the study of context. One of the arguments in his studies is that there is much interest in context and contextualization. Van Dijk proposes to define context in terms of context models in episodic memory, that is, in terms of subjective, dynamic representations of the ongoing communicative event and situation. It is these context models in cognition that, in van Dijk's view, control all discourse and communication, and especially all dimensions of discourse that adapt it to the current situation.

Van Dijk (1995) essentially perceives discourse analysis as ideology analysis, because according to him, "ideologies are typically, though not exclusively, expressed and reproduced in discourse and communication, including non-verbal semiotic messages, such as pictures, photographs and movies" (1995). For van Dijk, "ideologies... are the overall, abstract mental systems that organize... socially shared attitudes" (1995) and also "the basis of social representations shared by the members of a group" (1996). Therefore, the perceived identity of a group or a community belongs to the ideologies of this group. Ideologies, "indirectly influence the personal cognition of group members" in their act of comprehension of discourse among other actions and interactions (1995). He calls the mental representations of individuals during such social actions and interactions "models". For him, "models control how people act, speak or write, or how they understand the social practices of others" (1995). Of crucial importance here is that, according to van Dijk, mental representations "are often articulated along Us versus Them dimensions, in which speakers of one group will generally tend to present themselves or their own group in positive terms, and other groups in negative terms" (1995).

(2) Wodak's (1999) discourse-historical approach.

Ruth Wodak and her Vienna School base their modal on socio-linguistics in the Bernsteinian tradition, and on ideas of the Frankfurt school, especially those of Jŭrgen Habermas. Wodak conducted studies on institutional communication and speech barriers in court, schools, and in hospital clinics, and focused on sexism, contemporary anti-Semitism and racism in settings of various degrees of formality as well as on national and trans-national identity politics. The distinctive approach of Wodak and her colleagues is termed discourse-historical approach whose feature is its attempt to integrate systematically all available background information in the analysis and interpretation of the many layers of a written or spoken text. The study in which and for which this approach was developed attempted to trace in detail the constitution of an anti-Semitic stereotyped image as it emerged in public discourse in the 1986 Austrian presidential campaign of Kurt Waldheim. The study addressed the linguistic manifestations of prejudices towards Jews (Reisigl & Wodak, 2001; Wodak & Reisigl, 2002; Wodak, 2004; Pelinka & Wodak, 2002). More studies (Wodak & van Dijk, 2000; Blommaert & Verschueren, 1998) led the Vienna school to more general and theoretical considerations on the form and content of racist discourse about foreigners, indigenous minorities, immigrant workers, etc. More recently, Ruth Wodak has been concerned with investigating identity politics and patterns of decision-making in EU organizations. Fieldwork in European in "doing politics" "behind closed doors" (Muntigl, et al., 2000; Wodak & Weiss, 2005; Krzyzanowski, 2005; Oberhuber, 2005; Oberhuber, et al., 2005; Wodak, et al., 1999). In this research, together with either sociologists and political scientists, models were proposed to explain the context-dependent tensions and contradictions which necessarily arise in such a historically complex "entity" as Europe. EU officials were interviewed, policy documents analysed, political speeches on "a vision of Europe" collected, and media reporting on EU events confronted with the in-side view of EU organizations. The analysis of various genres illustrates the recontextualization of salient topoi and arguments in the transnational and national contexts.

Wodak (2001) summarizes the procedures of the discourse-historic approach to CDA:

—*Gather information about the co-and context of the text (social, political, historical, psychological, and so on).*

—*Establish the genre and discourse to which the text belongs, then sample more ethnographic information; locate texts on similar topics, texts with similar macro-topics, field of action, and genres.*

—*Formulate precise research questions and explore neighbouring fields for explanatory theories and other aspects that need to be considered.*

—*Operationalize the research questions into researchable linguistic categories.*

—*Apply these categories sequentially to the text using theoretical approaches to interpret the findings that result from the research questions.*

—*Draw up the context diagram for the specific text and the fields of actions.*

—*Make an extensive interpretation of the data, returning to the original research questions and the problem under investigation.*

This methodology aims to be pragmatic since the categories of analysis are developed in line with the research questions, with a constant movement back and forth between theory and empirical data. The historical context is always analysed and integrated into the interpretation, although there exists no stringent procedure for this task.

Thus to be in line with our present interdisciplinary research that should incorporate social, economic, political, cultural studies into the present linguistic discourse studies, the discourse-historical approach is adopted for its purpose in its attempting to integrate systematically all available background information in the analysis and interpretation of the many layers of discourse. In addition, our present research is a longitudinal one that should take historical changes into account. As Wodak (2001) points out that three concepts figure indispensably in all CDA: the concept of power, the concept of history and the concept of ideology, in this present research, we are to combine Wodak's discourse-historic and van Dijk's social-cognitive approaches in our analysis and interpretation of the present data. Therefore we place this research in the framework of CDA with an approach combining the discourse-historical and social-cognitive to the study of the data of the HK governments' PA pre- and post-transition.

### 2.2.6 Studies of national identity construction within the framework of CDA

(1) Wodak's (1999) study of Austrian identity construction.

Wodak, et al. (1999), in studying the discursive construction of national identity of Austrians, distinguish between three interrelated broad dimensions, which are respectively contents/topics, strategies, linguistic means and forms of realization.

*Contents/topics*

In a first dimension, a text may be examined as to its content. In other words, the manifest level of a text is of interest here, asking for what is apparently said or written. In her empirical research Wodak develops clusters, according to which she organises the various content-elements of a text. This matrix of thematic contents, consists all the topics primarily to the discursive construction of "national" identity which is based on the formation of sameness and difference. It is further divided into the following five major thematic areas:

i. the idea of a "homo austriacus" and a "homo externus";

ii. the narrative a collective political history;

iii. the discursive construction of a common culture;

iv. the discursive construction of a collective present and future;

v. the discursive construction of a "national body".

*Strategies*

Wodak (1999) employs the term "strategy" for the second dimension based on the notion of strategy by Heinemann and Viehwege (1991) —"thus it becomes clear that strategies mediate between communicative functions and objectives deduced from the interaction and the social condition of interacting partners and, on the other hand, the realization of linguistic (or extra-linguistic) means and their structuration". This second dimension is called "strategies of argumentation". In simple terms, strategies denote what the actors want. Any discursive action has an underlying strategy, be it conscious or unconscious. However, these strategies are not seen as purely finalistic and instrumental (Wodak, et al., 1990). She further distinguishes two kinds of strategies, namely, macro-strategies and micro-strategies.

i. macro-strategies include:

constructive strategies

perpetuation and justification strategies

transformation strategies

dismantling or destructive strategies

(Note: Wodak further attributes many sub-strategies to these four macro-strategies, of which we will employ some that are useful to the present research.)

ii. micro-strategies include:

presupposing intra-national sameness or similarity

emphasizing national singularity

the presupposition or emphasis of differences between nations

positive self-presentation

negative other-presentation

*Linguistic means and forms of realization*

Discourse analysis according to Wodak has to be complemented by a third perspective, namely the analysis of a text's linguistic realisations. Here one searches for linguistic characteristics on the level of single words, of sentences and of the text as a whole. This third dimension focuses primarily on lexical units and syntactic devices which serve to construct unification, unity, sameness, difference, uniqueness, origin and so on. The three broad categories are as follows:

i. personal reference (anthroponymic generic terms, personal pronouns, quantifiers);

ii. spatial reference (toponyms/geonyms, adverbs of place, spatial reference through persons, by means of prepositional phrases such as "with us" "with them");

iii. temporal reference (temporal prepositions, adverbs of time, temporal conjunctions, temporal references by means of nouns, semi-prefixes with temporal meaning).

Wodak adopts this three-dimension framework in her analysis of narrative discourse in public, political and media areas as well as in semi-private and quasi-private areas. As the data of the present research focuses on the instutitionalized genre of the governments' Policy Address, we could only adopt some of the notions in this framework. As Wodak (2001) states, constructive strategies were used more in the political speeches than in all other data. To create and enhance identity through discursive acts is, of course, the job of every politician, but especially of those who presume to speak for a large imagined community. Thus, the present research focuses only on the constructive aspect of the HK governments' PA with the view that the other three strategies of perpetuation, transformation and destruction are of less significance in the present case. Therefore, the second dimension in Wodak's framework converges into only one strategy of construction in the present research.

In Wodak's study, the third dimension researches only on the linguistic realizations of the strategies. Notwithstanding the fact that linguistic variations are numerous and linguistic analysis may focus on very different aspects of language—phonetics or morphology for example—linguistic analysis for our purposes is not quite as complex, because it may be built upon the work done by the specialists. The present author of this research considers that the linguistic aspects of the constructive strategy could not satisfy the present research goals and some other aspects should be taken into consideration like the pragmatic and intertextual aspects of the discourse.

(2) Ricento's (2003) study of Americanism with a revised framework.

Ricento (2003) focuses his study on the construction of American national identity which emerged during the Americanization campaign, roughly 1914—1924 which is really a short period of time but significant in that the early European colonizers (mainly religious dissidents form Northern Europe) were interested in separating themselves, physically and philosophically, from many aspects of their European histories and in creating a new "American" identity in language, dress, social life, world view, and so on. In such a process a distinct American identity was conceptualized out of the desire of the colonizers' breaking from European traditions and of establishing a new race of people on a continent in which they were for many decades a minority group. Period texts are analyzed using techniques of pragmatic and rhetorical analysis within a discourse-historical framework which is based on Wodak's (1999) and two types of strategies are distinguished in the construction of Americanism, of which one is rhetorical strategies used as plans to achieve certain political, psychological or other kinds of objectives in shaping thinking and persuading readers, and the other type is linguistic strategies. Three representations of Americanism are described. Two of these representations presuppose consensus on particular views of American identity, whereas the third finds such views to be narrow-minded and incompatible with the goals of democracy. The two strategies in his analyzing framework are following:

①rhetorical strategies.

i. Constructive Strategies, which "attempt to construct and to establish a certain national identity by promoting unification, identification and solidarity, as well as differentiation. Three sub-groups under Constructive Strategies are:

a. the group of strategies of justification which attempts to justify of relativize a societal status quo ante;

b. strategies of unification and cohesivation which emphasize unifying common features and inclusion;

c. strategy of avoidance which suppresses/backgrounds intra-national differences and discontinuities/disruptions.

ii. strategies of transformation which "aim to transform a relatively well established national identity and its components into another identity".

iii. strategies of perpetuation presuppose and/or emphasize positive political continuity. A sub-strategy in this category is: strategy of avoidance which seeks to suppress or circumvent the issue of change.

②linguistic strategies.

i. use of personal pronouns (especially first person) in order to establish in-group/out-group membership, among other things;

ii. verb tense and aspect, and other types of temporal reference;

iii. vagueness in referential or other expressions, including euphemisms, allusions, rhetorical questions, and passive constructions;

iv. the suppression of agency by use of passives and other linguistic means, as well as the mis-assignment of agency;

v. tropes of metonymy (the name of a referent is replaced with the name of an entity with which it is closely associated), synecdoche (replaces the name of a referent with the name of another referent which belongs to the same semantic field), and personification (a human form is attributed to an abstract entity).

Ricento's (2003) framework is a two-fold, which is simpler compared with Wodak's, for he also omitted an important part in Wodak's framework, the content or the topics that construct national identity. Ricento's study also differs from Wodak's in that the data in this study were works of some influential elites because not everyone can get published in the mainstream media and nor can just anyone hold forth the floor of the U. S. Congress to discuss his or her views about a particular issue. Ricento thus concentrates on three texts of power elites who command the most attention and whose views are most pervasive in the hegemonic construction of mainstream American identity.

But the significance of his study lies in that he proves Wodak's framework can also be used to analyse the discursive construction of other national identity besides that of the Austrian in Wodak's work. Furthermore, the study of discourse of socially valued resources, like political discourse of the government's PA, proves to be more penetrative because the producers of such discourse have social power to greater access to the tools of persuasion by which they can use strategies to "change the mind of others in one's own interests" (van Dijk, 1993).

(3) Flowerdew's (2004) discursive strategies in identity construction.

Flowerdew (2004) in his study of the discourse of Hong Kong's first Chief Executive, based on a corpus of primarily speeches, but also interviews, press conferences and other pronouncements, media reports and commentary, compares the discursive strategies of Tung Chee-Hwa, the first Chief Executive of Hong Kong and those of Chris Patten, the last British colonial Governor of Hong Kong in the discursive construction of identity. He claims that the four core elements of Chris Patten's discursive strategies which Flowerdew (1997) categorized have remained in Tung Chee-Hwa's speech, with emphasis shifting. The four discursive strategies are:

i. the transformation of old political genres and the introduction of new ones;

ii. presupposition;

iii. involvement (the use of indexicals);

iv. lexical structuring and reiteration.

With the four discursive strategies, Tung Chee-Hwa emphasizes more on the knowledge-based economy with regard to the free market, but downplaying the role of democratic development. In addition, the notions of the Hong Kong people as believers in Confucian values and their essential Chineseness have been emphasized in an attempt to establish a new identity for the people of Hong Kong. Flowerdew continues to emphasize that Tung has not been very effective in his construction of the new HK identity because his popularity ratings suggest that people do not agree with him.

Flowerdew's four strategies may shed light on the present research, but his study is considered not a very systematic one because a lot of extemporaneous speeches are involved which may be taken as personal opinions of the CE, while the present research tries to examine the stance or voice of the HK government instead of the individual speeches because the PA is considered to be the work of a group of people and also well-prepared (which will be further justified in Chapter 3). And the effectiveness of these discursive strategies is not the focus of the present research which tries to answer how the two governments construct the identity for their people.

(4) Dra. Elaine Hewitt's (2006).

The study of Dra. Elaine Hewitt, who is a student of R. Wodak, is her unpublished PHD dissertation on the discursive construction of Gibraltarian identity in the printed discourse. She follows Wodak's framework in the studying of a new context of Gibraltar in three corpora of editorials in newspapers in Gibraltar, Spain and Britain. In this study, she combines the analytical categories of the discourse-historical approach, namely, the referential and predicational strategies, with the transitivity system in SFL to provide a systematic analysis. Because the very typical genre of editorials, she abandons many other strategies in Wodak' s discourse-historical CDA with the exception of referential and predicational strategies, which sheds light on our present research on the particular genre of the governments' PA that the discourse-historical CDA is a tool box from which we can draw the analytical tools that are applicable to this present research, and when the tools in the discourse-historical CDA are not adequate for the present data, we can enrich our own tool kit by complementing it from other perspectives.

The above review of the related identity studies within the framework of CDA shows that there are gaps needed to fill in this present research. CDA is proved to be an effective approach to the study of identity, but it is not yet evident that it can be used in a detailed and systematic comparative analysis of HK identity. Furthermore, we found that the analytical tools in the framework in the previous studies are not adequate for an analysis of political discourse study. Therefore, it is necessary and significant to work out a framework that is operational and practicable in political discourse of the government's PA.

### 2.2.7 Intertextuality

The notion of intertextuality is not taken into account in the reviewed studies of discursively constructed national identity in the previous section. Though it has received slight attention in the discursive construction of identity, it permeates through language and needs detailed investigation and review.

During the "transitional period" from structuralism to post structuralism (in the late 1960s), Kristeva (1986, actually written in 1966) coined the term "intertextuality". For Kristeva, intertextuality implies "the insertion of history (society) into a text and of this text into history" (1986). Based upon Kristeva's expression of intertextuality, the French discourse analysts (Authier-Revus, 1982; Maingueneau, 1987) draw a distinction between "manifest" and "constitutive" intertextuality. The latter is highlighted by Fairclough as "interdiscursivity" in order to echo Peheux's (1982) notion of "interdiscourse" and to foreground various elements of "orders of discourse" such as genres, discourse and styles. According to Fairclough, all texts are intertextual, in sense that text contains within itself evidences of the histories of other texts. Scholars in different fields approach the notion of "intertextuality" from different perspectives for different purposes. These scholars could be roughly categorized into two groups.

The first group is the scholars from semiotics, mainly from so-called literary semiotics including Kristeva (1981), Bakhtin (1981, 1986), Frow (1986), Collins (1989), Culler (1981), Bradford (1997), Meinhof & Smith (2000), Allen (2000) and Chandler (2005). These scholars concern themselves with exploring the complex and heterogeneous nature of literary works by appropriating the concept of intertextuality. Of these studies, the most detailed exploration of intertextuality is found in Bradford's (1997) Stylitics, where Bradford applies his theory of "double pattern" to the analysis of genre mixing and/or genre switching in poetry, novel and drama. Bradford ascribes intertextuality to the political and social disorders at that time. "Practically all of Shakespeare's plays are composed of two very different stylistic patterns: verse and unversified speech. We can make a number of reasonably straightforward observations about the reason for using blank verse and prosaic speech in the same text. Often the distinction between blank verse and prose mirrors the distinction between social status and behavioral patterns of the characters" (Bradford, 1997). This view helps us better understand the macro relationship between literature and social/historical context but fails to reveal in depth the operating process of intertextuality and does not take the dynamics of communication into consideration.

The second group is from the area of discourse analysis and critical discourse analysis, such as Fairclough (1992a, b, c, 1995a, b, 2003a), Bhatia (1995, 1997, 2004), Scollon (1998, 2000, 2002, 2004), Bazerman (1993, 2004), Devitt (1991), Beaugrande & Dressler (1981), Lemke (1983, 1985, 1988a, b, 1995a, b), Xin (2000), Wodak (2001) and White (2002). For this group of scholars, their major concern is with non-literary works. Many scholars perceive intertextuality not only as a form through which texts are interrelated, but also as a social practice that involves particular socially regulated ways of producing and interpreting discourse which can contribute a lot to the changes in social identity (Fairclough, 1992a, b, c, 1995b, 2003a). It bridges the gap between linguistic analysis and social research by scrutinizing the social and critical significance of intertextuality, especially those intertextual phenomena that are located in instituational settings, such as political, commercial, educational, medicating, mediating and mass media, etc. This attempt has brought the dynamics of communication back into the studies of interdiscursivity through analyzing the discursive practices staged within the linguistically implied arenas. Fairclough (1992a) holds that modern societies are characterized by a tendency towards increasing control over more and more parts of people's lives, producing various kinds of public-private genre mixing and public discourse are "conversationalized". He also claims that intertextuality reflects the three interlocking tendencies of contemporary discourse—democratization, marketization, and technologization, which are part of the wider process of social changes. Bhatia (2004) offers a detailed account of intertextuality in terms of the increasing hybridization of organizational life, and presents an analysis of the application potential of genre mixtures. While Scollon (1998, 2000, 2002) employs intertextual analysis in his identity study in news discourse in Hong Kong. Thus, it is clear that intertextuality, as well as the constantly changing intertextual relations in texts, is central to an understanding of the process of social change. Bazerman (2004) states further that "intertextuality is not just a matter of which other texts you refer to, but how you use them, what you use them for, and ultimately how you position yourself as a writer to them to make your own statement". Bazerman further puts forward basic concepts and a procedure of analysing intertextuality. The basic concepts he describes include levels of intertextuality, techniques of intertextual representation, intertextual distance or reach, and translation across contexts/recontextualization. The basic procedure Bazerman (2004) outlines can be briefly summarised as follows.

—*Identify your purpose for doing intertextual analysis and what questions you hope to answer by doing it*;
—*Identify the specific texts you want to examine*; *in other words*, *identify your corpus*;
—*Identify the traces of other texts by examining explicit overt references to other authors*;
—*Start making observations and interpretations by considering the reference in relation to the context of what the author is saying*;
—*Look for more subtle clues to cater for your analytical purpose*;
—*Start looking for a pattern from which you can start developing a conclusion.*

In this present study, the CDA approach to intertextuality together with Bazerman's procedure is preferred to the stylistic approach out of the several considerations. First, the CDA approach can help to explain what social changes discourse reflects and why. Second, the CDA approach takes the socio-cultural contexts into consideration which fits in with the purpose of this study. Last, the CDA approach focuses more on non-literary discourse.

## 2.3 The perspective of the present study

The above review shows that the previous studies on identity construction have made great contribution to the understanding of this sociolinguistic issue of identity. The major findings obtained so far have provided us with the basis to the study of the identity problem in HK. However, the existing researches still have some limitations, and more efforts are needed to further the exploration of the co-variation of discursive identity construction with the socio-political change. The present study serves as a CDA research in the context of HK, as a contribution to a systematic and coherent interpretation of this sociolinguistic phenomenon in the HK governments' PA, a highly institutionalized genre of political discourse. It is to be carried out in the following three aspects:

Firstly, with the focus on the only genre of PA, the present study attempts to generate an analytical framework based on Wodak's (1999) three-dimensioned framework which has been employed in the national identity construction in different genres. In accordance with Wodak's (2006) view that a CDA study should draw from different branches of linguistics, the present study will root its framework in Wodak's and make revisions and adaptations to it from theories of pragmatics and intertextuality and approach the HK identity construction in more details by looking into all social, cultural, political as well as cognitive factors involved in the discourse of PA.

Secondly, the two different approaches to CDA, van Dijk's social-cognitive and Wodak's discourse-historical, are not mutually exclusive, rather, the present author considers them to be rather complementary. In view of this, the present study will integrate the two approaches in our analysis and interpretation of the present data.

Finally, although previous studies have analysed the discursive construction of national or community identities, no study that is systematic and comprehensive is set in the context of HK and takes into account of the comparison between the pre-transitional PA and post-transitional PA. Therefore, the present study basically attempts to make such a comparison in order to better understand the co-variation between the discursive identity construction and socio-political change of the transition of HK sovereignty.

## 2.4 A summary

This chapter has highlighted the notion of identity and the theoretical frameworks in the area of critical discourse analysis and intertextuality that inform and provide guidelines for the study, with the purpose to offer a brief review of the sociolinguistic issue of identity in CDA. The first part sketches the terminological issue and the different manifestations of identity and HK identity. The second part, specifically, has outlined Wodak's three-dimensional modal for identity construction and CDA approach to intertextuality which provides a basis for the analytical framework of the present study. In addition, this part has reviewed the major theoretical principles in CDA as an approach to research and the two approaches of social-cognitive and discourse-historical in doing

CDA. The above theories and the major findings of studies from different perspectives lay down the foundation of the present research. With the merits and demerits of the past research clarified, we introduce our own perspective of this study and are on the way to generate an analytical framework for the present research.

The following chapter will put the theoretical frameworks reviewed together and present the research methodology employed in the present study. It will also discuss the principles of the research design, data collection and the data analysis procedures used in the study.

# Chapter 3 Research Framework

The previous chapter has offered a brief review of the theories of identity, CDA and intertextuality and relevant studies in these theories, which has laid a solid foundation for the construction of an analytical framework for the present research. The purpose of this chapter is to present a description and explanation of the theoretical framework which has been developed from a preliminary analysis of data collected for the present study. It commences with proposing a research question—based on the present data and related theories—of the present study. Then follows a brief description and justification of the data collected for this research. Finally, the analytical and theoretical frameworks are presented for the present analysis of the discursive identity construction with relevant theories that will be applied to analyse the present data and tackle the research question and to help interpret the discursive construction of HK identity in the two HK governments' PA.

## 3.1 Research question

The purpose of the present research, based on Critical Discourse Analysis, by looking into the 22 Policy Addresses of the two Hong Kong governments', is to investigate the sociolinguistic issue of the discursive construction of HK identity in the Policy Address and uncover the co-variation between the discursive construction of identities and socio-political change of the transition. Therefore, the present research is to address the research question as follows:

*How are the two distinct identities of Hong Kong people discursively constructed in the Policy Address of the Hong Kong governments, before and after the transition of HK sovereignty that took place in 1997?*

In order to address the above research question, some operational definitions of the research question are offered as follows:

(1) *HK identity refers to the identity of the HK citizens who held British Dependent Territories Citizen passport and were considered to be "British citizens" before the* 1997 *transition of HK sovereignty from Britain to China, and who are "Chinese citizens in HK" according to the Basic Law after the* 1997 *transition.* ①

(2) *Policy Address, or PA, refers to the speech delivered annually by either the HK Governor of the British Colonial Government before the transition or the Chief Executive (CE) of the HKSAR Government after the Transition of HK sovereignty from Britain to China to the Legislative Council, giving a conclusion of the work of the previous year and setting goals and plans for the coming year.*

(3) *Discursive identity construction refers to the identity constructed by means of language, particularly in discourses of the two HK governments' PA which is a highly institutionalized genre in political discourse.*

(4) *HK governments indicate the British Colonial HK Government before* 1997 *Transition and the Government of the Hong Kong Special Administrative Region after 1997.*

(5) *The transition of HK sovereignty signifies the end of the British rule over HK, in which British transferred the sovereignty of HK to China on July 1st, 1997.*

## 3.2 Description of the data in the present study

### 3.2.1 Data collection

The data to be analyzed in the present study consists of the 11 annual Policy Addresses delivered by the HKSAR Government from the year 1997 to 2008, (actually there should have been 12 PAs, but the year 2002 was the year of election, so this year's PA was postponed to the beginning of 2003, thus there are 11 PAs) and in order

① Basic Law can be referred to http://www.cmab.gov.hk/en/issues/basic2.htm#1.

to keep a balance in analyses and comparisons, the other 11 annual Policy Addresses right before the 1997 Transition by the British Colonial Hong Kong Government spanning from the year 1986 to 1996. The former 11 were obtained from the web of annual Policy Addresses of the HKSAR Government and the latter 11 were drawn and copied from the Chongji Library in Hong Kong Chinese University. Altogether 22 texts are involved in the present research and a corpus of the 22 PAs is set up consisting of a sub-corpus of the pre-transition PA and another of the post-transition PA. It is assumed that a total of 22 PAs will be sufficient to provide a solid basis for a significant analysis of the discursive construction of HK identity and a detailed comparison of the two governments' PAs.

### 3. 2. 2 Data justification

#### 3. 2. 2. 1 Power in Policy Address

In the review of related literature of identity studies, it is evident that the studies differ to a great degree in their research data in that Wodak (1999) studies different types of talk varying from the very public of political speeches to the very private of personal chat, that Ricento (2003) studies the three pieces of writing of the elites, that Flowerdew (2004) studies the talks of the HK Governor and the HKSAR CE, and Dra. and that Elaine Hewitt (2006) studies reports in different press. In this study, the British HK Governors' or the HKSAR Chief Executive's annual PA is studied, because those who have social power have greater access to the tools of persuasion (e. g. , the media, political office) by which they can use strategies to change the mind of others in their own interests, as van Dijk (1993) has pointed out that "social power is based on privileged access to socially valued resources, such as wealth, income, position, status, force, group membership, education or knowledge". One of the major functions of dominant discourse (that is, the discourse of the dominant group or power), as Herman & Chomsky (1988) demonstrate, is to manufacture consensus about and acceptance of their dominance. Therefore, a study concentrating on the discourse of PA by the British HK Governors or the HKSAR CEs is most appropriate because such people command the most attention (by virtue of their privileged access to ways in which to air their views) and whose views are most influential in the hegemonic construction of HK identity.

#### 3. 2. 2. 2 Policy Address as the voice of the government

The PA of the HK governments has been considered to be a very important voice of the HK governments and to possess the broadest channels in preaching the mainstream ideologies owing to the power in the discourse.

The authors of speeches cannot be assumed to be the "animators"—to use Goffman's (1981) term—that is the politicians who deliver a speech—is also the persons who actually write it. Ultimately it may not be of great importance whether the speakers actually write the texts of their speeches themselves, which is highly unlikely considering the workload of current politicians, especially the highest political representatives of a state, or merely take part in its composition, because the person who delivers the speech is always solely responsible for its content. According to Kammerer (1995), writers of speeches, together with political advisors, contribute considerably to the production of all the texts—about 160 speeches plus contributions to newspapers and journals and several hundred personal letters—that politicians produce a year. No one with even a vague knowledge of the workload of a president or an executive would seriously believe that he himself writes all these speeches himself. However, the increasing personalization of politics forces politicians to conceal the origin of their speeches from the public and to obscure the fact that top political offices, such as those of the President, the Chancellor, or cabinet ministers, necessitate large teams with corporate identity status, of which speechwriters are important members. The question of authorship will concern us only marginally and we will no longer distinguish between the politicians as speakers and the authors of the speeches.

The CE or the Governor is the head of the community and hence the supreme representative of HK, both internally and abroad. As the community "preacher" and a kind of voice in the community, the CE or the Governor is expected to address issues deemed important to the state in a solemn, dignified manner on relevant occasions (Welan, 1995) and ideally, to act as an integrative authority to promote harmony and to defuse potential conflicts. The CE's/Governor's actions primarily consist of talking and he is therefore evaluated mainly by his words (Kammerer, 1995). Thus we assumed that the speeches would most strongly aim at consistently creating identity and unity and would neglect intra-national (or intra-regional) differences as much as possible, or would present them in such a way as not to inhibit the generation of a feeling of national identification. For this purpose, the executive would primarily select and favour those linguistic means of realization which implicitly or explicitly expresse(d) sameness, similarity, unity and solidarity. And also the executive would primarily stress continuity and stability for the future—an essential component of sameness—and where changes seemed necessary, cautious strategies of transformation would be used.

#### 3.2.2.3 Policy Address as an institutionalized genre of political discourse

Language and politics are social stances; the one, a medium used by society for the purposes of communication and cohabitation, the other, loosely, the ideas and activities used for gaining and exercising power in society. As such a linguistic study of political language, that which we intend to do here, conflates the social components of the two stances. It is van Dijk's (2004) characterization of the field of politics that establishes, most succinctly, politics as discourse:

> *... this field may briefly—and some what traditionally be defined by its overall systems (democracy, dictatorship), special social macro actions, such as government, legislation, elections, or decision making, ... micro practices, interactions or discourses, such as parliamentary debates, canvassing or demonstrations, ... special social relations, such as those of institutional power, ... special norms and values (e. g. freedom, equality etc.) ... political cognitions, such as political ideologies (van Dijk's,* 2004).

In accordance with van Dijk's (2004) definition of political discourse, the HK government's PA is considered to be a typical type of political discourse, a social action of the HK government.

Politics is thus a discursive domain, not just because it situates language in action but also because the action is contextualised. The use of linguistic parameters for interpreting political language is a fairly recent enterprise. According to Wilson (1990), Geis (1987) is the first complete textbook written by any linguist on political language. Ever since, however, linguists have devoted considerable attention to political discourse: Wilson (1990), from the point of view of linguistic pragmatics, Cap (2002) from an eclectic linguistic angle of vision, and Chilton (2004), from the discourse-analytic perspective, to mention but a few.

Political discourse analysis studies political text and talk, i. e. communicative acts which have "a direct functional role as a form of political action in the political process" (van Dijk, 1997) and which are performed by political actors, mostly but not only "professional politicians... such as presidents and prime ministers and other members of government, parliament or political parties" (van Dijk, 1997). One of the principal goals of political discourse analysis, according to Wilson (2001), is to identify the many ways in which language can be used or manipulated by political actors to produce specific effects in the political realm. It also tries to establish a link between language and political science. The study of political discourse analysis thus should adopt what van Dijk (1997) has called an "integrated approach". It goes beyond a purely language-based analysis of the speeches in so far as it also examines the functionality of the observed discursive practices in their wider political context. Consequently, the present study of the HK governments' PA should not only constitute a contribution to political discourse analysis but also to political science, as it considers why, within the given political context, specific linguistic choices have been made and attempts to map these discursive patterns or practices onto political actions and goals.

Chilton (2004) asserts that "politics is very largely the use of language". Butt, et al. (2004) make a similar albeit somewhat stronger claim when they write that "the very use of language is ideological". They argue that this is so because "the use of language necessitates choices between different modes of meaning". It is precisely these choices, that are simply unavoidable during a communicative act and have to be made at all levels (semantic, syntactic, lexical and so on) of language, that can be used by political actors to political effect, as Wilson (2001) pointed out. The political plasticity of language has the potential to turn language into a "fearsome resource", argues Hasan (1996), a resource "through which we not only do seemingly trivial things (...) but through [which] we can also have the power of doing enormously momentous things". Indeed, Hasan (1996) adds, "we not only use language to shape reality, but we use it also to defend that reality, against anyone whose alternative values might threaten ours". This is the highly plastic side of political discourse in its operation of differing choices of linguistic devices. Thus in our political discourse analysis, another goal is to see how language is manipulative with the different choices of linguistic devices at different levels.

Another notion that concerns the present study and is of the same portion of importance is genre, which is defined and identified differently from diversified perspectives. Genre, according to Martin and others, is held to be a staged, goal-oriented social process (Martin, 1993; Martin, 2001; Martin & Rose, 2003), "social because we participate in genres with other people; goal-oriented because we use genres to get things done; staged because it usually takes us a few steps to reach our goals" (Martin & Rose, 2003). Fairclough (2003) adopts a critical linguistic stance to the conception of genre: a genre is a specifically discoursal aspect of ways of acting and interacting in the course of social events. Genres can be highly abstract such as Narrative or Report and can be rather concrete such as job interview as well. They can also be tied to particular networks of social practices such as political interview in contemporary television. "... the genres associated with a particular network of social practices constitute a potential which is variably drawn upon in actual texts and interaction." (Fairclough, 2003). Thus, genre is established as social activities with communicative needs, and it is context-dependent and purpose-driven and mostly discoursal.

The Hong Kong governments' Policy Address is an annual speech delivered by the Hong Kong Governor pre-transition or the Chief Executive of the HKSAR Government to the Legislative Council of the Hong Kong governments at the end of each year. It usually contains a review of the past year and lays down plans for the coming year and sets longer-term goals for the future in the fields of politics, economy and cultural living of this region. Though it is delivered by the Governor or the Chief Executive alone, it is rather the voice of the government than this individual. Thus it is context-dependent and purpose-driven and discoursal. As a special genre of political discourse, the Policy Address not only signals some of the most important political, social and cultural events and aspects of Hong Kong, but also are essentially hortatory with the primary function of getting people to do things under the ruling of the government and especially in the service of indoctrinating the Hong Kong people with the mainstream political ideology. As a highly institutionalized genre, it is predictable that it does not vary considerably over time in schematic structure, which is the invariable side of this highly institutionalized genre.

Therefore, our present study of the identity construction in the HK governments' PA is defined as the study of the plastic linguistic operation of the invariable institutionalized genre.

### 3.2.3 Data description

Thus the present data is composed of two sub-corpora—one consists of the eleven PAs before the transition of the British Colonial HK Government, the other of the eleven PAs after the transition of the HKSAR Government. Thus, the total number of words of the whole corpus is 292 185, with the first sub-corpora of the PAs before the transition 149 178 words and the other sub-corpora of the PAs after the transition 143 025 words. Taken the quantity of words into consideration, the present two sub-corpora are considered to be paralleled so that they are comparable. The total number of words of the 22 PAs are as follows:

**Table 2 The total number of words of the 22 Policy Addresses**

| Year of PA | Total No. of words | Year of PA | Total No. of words |
|---|---|---|---|
| 1986 | 11 356 | 1997 | 15 027 |
| 1987 | 15 732 | 1998 | 18 193 |
| 1988 | 16 695 | 1999 | 18 879 |
| 1989 | 11 835 | 2000 | 14 030 |
| 1990 | 11 695 | 2001 | 12 889 |
| 1991 | 7 527 | 2003 | 7 796 |
| 1992 | 15 253 | 2004 | 8 596 |
| 1993 | 18 040 | 2005 | 11 505 |
| 1994 | 11 927 | 2006 | 89 74 |
| 1995 | 18 043 | 2007 | 14 866 |
| 1996 | 11 075 | 2008 | 12 270 |
| Total words of the PA pre-transition | 149 178 | Total words of the PA post-transition | 143 025 |

## 3.3 Analytical and theoretical frameworks

### 3.3.1 General description

The present study is to be carried out mainly as a qualitative one complemented with some statistics data, combining the descriptive, explanative and interpretative approaches. It is assumed that a corpus-based study might be more revealing in defining the more inherent nature of national identity or community identity. Based upon the brief review of the relevant literature, the study formulates the research question in relation to identity construction in the Hong Kong governments' annual Policy Addresses and then tries to answer this question through a careful analysis of the selected data and the socio-cultural factors beyond them.

Ruud (2003) argues that a quantitative analysis of political text and talk "cannot tell the whole story". In her view, a critical qualitative analysis of the linguistic patterns selected by political actors is a more convenient way of demonstrating how these patterns reflect the conceptualisations of politicians. Citing van Dijk's (1993) multidisciplinary approach to CDA, an approach within discourse analysis which is frequently adopted by political discourse analysts, she adds that the mapping of the micro-level linguistic properties of a communicative act onto macro-level phenomena in the political realm leads to a better understanding of the functionality of these linguistic properties in political discourse.

The present study is a case of corpus-supported critical discourse analysis. Stubbs (1996) suggests that a corpus-based approach to CDA can help overcome one of the perceived weaknesses of CDA: the lack of substantive empirical support for some of its claims. In the past decade, increasing numbers of CDA studies have been appearing which drew on specialized corpora which analysts compiled themselves. Flowerdew (1997) examined the discourse of the colonial withdrawal from Hong Kong, with claims substantiated by corpus data. Fairclough (2000) did a keywords analysis of the discourse of the Labour Party in Britain under Tony Blair's leadership, using the corpus technique of keywords analysis (Scott, 1997; Scott & Tribble, 2006), in which a computer program compares two corpora to generate a list of words whose differential frequencies of use are statistically significant. In a similar vein, Teubert (2000) looked at keywords in the discourse of "Eurpscepticism" in Britain, and Partington (2003) analysed the linguistic characteristics of political argument, a process he termed "Corpus-Assisted Discourse Studies". David Y. W. Lee (2008) even predicts that the way corpora were used in these will become more or less standard for CDA studies in the future.

Thus we consider that an integrative approach of qualitative supplemented with statistics drawn from the corpus would be more revealing in our description, explanation and interpretation of the present research questions.

Concerning the notion of discursive strategies, Wodak (1999) employs the term "strategy" for the second dimension in her framework based on the notion of strategy by Heinemann and Viehwege (1991) —"thus it becomes clear that strategies mediate between communicative functions and objectives deduced from the interaction and the social condition of interacting partners and, on the other hand, the realization of linguistic (or extra-linguistic) means and their structuration" . In our present study, the only communicative function or objective analysed is the construction of HK identity in the discursive practice of the governments' PA. Thus, in this research, discursive strategy refers to any means or aspect that contributes to the construction of HK identity in the discursive practice of the governments' PA.

### 3.3.2 Analytical framework

The review of relevant literature in Chapter 2 has presented the theoretical background that provides the necessary framework for the present research, covering three important aspects: the HK identity paradigm, the critical discourse analysis paradigm, and the discursive construction of national identity. This present research does not intend to feature nor to solve the political problem of HK. Its aim is to analyse and interpret what discursive strategies are employed in the HK governments' Policy Address and how HK identity is constructed in this genre with three forces at play: the Britain government, the Chinese government, and the HK government, and how this genre of HK governments' PA spread and impose certain political and social beliefs, values and perspectives, shaping society's perception on a particular issue, namely the identity of HK.

Moreover, from the variety of approaches mentioned that lie under the common umbrella of CDA, the present piece of research is to be placed within an analytical framework under the discourse-historical approach as described and developed by Wodak. (Wodak, et al., 1999; Wodak & Meyer, 2001; Reisigl & Wodak, 2001). This approach has proved particularly useful for the study of historical and political topics as it—in an interdisciplinary way—integrates a vast amount of background historical information combined with socio-political and linguistic perspectives. In addition, the discourse-historical approach has been successfully applied in pieces of research which share similar goals to the ones that concern the present research here, i. e., the analysis of the discursive construction of national or collective identities. Thus, the discourse-historical approach can provide the appropriate framework for the study of the discursive construction of HK identity.

In investigating such complex issues, the discourse-historical approach "attempts to integrate a large quantity of available knowledge about the historical sources and background of the social and political fields in which discursive "events" are embedded (Wodak, 2001a), together with the incorporation of the appropriate social theories to explain the context. This model, is thus essentially similar to the practice of other critical discourse analysts, but with a special emphasis on the analysis of the historical context, to integrate it into the interpretation of discourses, and the incorporation of ethnography to explore from the inside the object under investigation. In other words, it is particularly historically-oriented and context-sensitive.

As has been discussed in the previous chapter, discourse is socially constituted and at the same time it is socially constitutive, i. e., it influences the social institutions and social settings in which the discursive act appears. In addition, according to the findings of the discourse-historical approach, in so doing, discourse fulfils four main functions: constructive function, perpetuating function, transformative function and destructive function (Wodak, 2001a). In other words, discourse can help to construct, justify, change and dismantle a certain social condition or situation, respectively. Though these four functions in Wodak's study are named macro-strategies—constructive strategy, preservative strategy, transformative strategy and destructive strategy, the present author considers them as four functions of language and tries to investigate the systematic ways of using language to achieve a particular aim—constructive function in the HK governments' PA. Thus, in Wodak's 3-dimension framework becomes two-layer in this research, because the second layer in her framework—the four macro-strategies are converted into one—construction function of language in the present framework.

The major concern of the present study, as stated above, is to study discursive construction of Hong Kong identity in the governments' Policy Address. Therefore, our purpose is to formulate a model for analyzing identities discursively constructed in the Policy Address. To do so, we have to re-categorize the linguistic resources involved in the previously discussed model along the following two dimensions: what topics are included in the construction of national identity and how the identity is constructed. Based on the previous theoretical frameworks, our present model will be a two-dimensioned framework—macro-strategies and micro-strategies. The macro-strategies are to answer the question of what topics are included, or what is chosen to be addressed in the PAs, while the micro-strategies are to answer the question of how the strategies in different levels of the discourse are employed in the construction of different identities.

As has been mentioned, CDA draws on many different theoretical frameworks to carry out the textual analysis. Following van Dijk's suggestion about not following a single expert in the practice of CDA (2001) and based on the results of prior studies on the HK identity, the present author works out the following model for the present study. Consequently the methodological model developed for the present research has been adapted from the approach and categories of analysis described by Wodak, et al. (1999) and complemented with theories from pragmatics and intertextuality.

HK identity is constructed in terms of its relations to China. One identity needs "others" to define itself since it is the "others" who make it possible to establish the difference. According to van Dijk (1973), the out-group is often delegitimised and the in-group is often legitimized, or the out-group is devalued and the in-group is valued. This analytical framework in the present study takes a two-step process. At first, the distinction between the in-group/self and out-group/others is drawn through an analysis of the macro-strategies. The macro-strategies aim to answer the question of what content or topics are addressed in the PA in order to construct the in-group vs. the out-group. The second step is an analysis of the attachment of different values to the two groups—in-group with positive labels and out-group with negative labels, through the use of micro-strategies. Another function of the micro-strategies is also to answer the question of what linguistic devices are employed and how they are employed in the PA to attach the differing values to the in-group and out-group.

Macro-strategies refer to the topics employed to establish a certain community identity by promoting intra-community sameness, similarity, unification, identification and solidarity, as well as the presupposition or emphasis of differences with other communities. They consist of:

*a content analysis of*

*the discursive construction of common politics*

*the discursive construction of a common economy*

*the discursive construction of a common culture*

*a topic analysis of*

*some topics that are prominently in contrast in the two sub-corpora in the discursive construction of HK identity.*

Micro-strategies refer to the use of different linguistic devices with varying degree of elaborateness in the discursive construction of Hong Kong identity. We distinguish three types of sub-strategies of micro-strategies in language use—referential, rhetorical and intertextual as follows:

*Referential strategies*: *personal references*
*temporal references*
*spatial references*
*Rhetorical strategies*: *allusion*
*presupposition*
*Intertextual strategy*: *intertextuality*

The analytical framework of the discursive construction of HK identities in the present study, consisting of the macro-strategies and micro-strategies can be illustrated in the following figure:

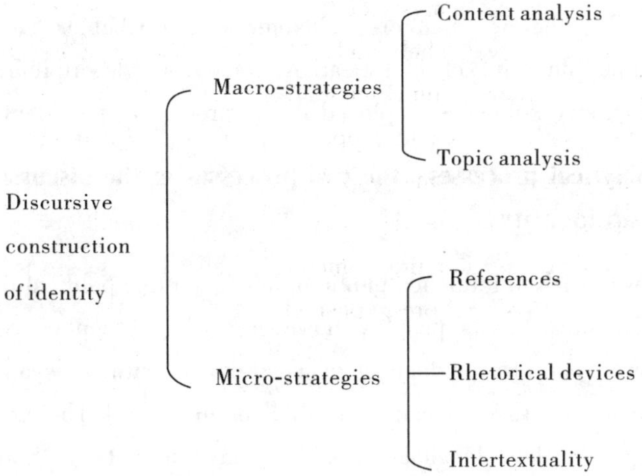


In this analytical framework, macro-strategies are strategies used to establish "in-group" and "out-group" with the concepts of sameness and difference.

*The content analysis shows the "in-group" commonness and sameness in three aspects of economy, politics and culture.*

*The topic analysis shows the "in-group" commonness and sameness as well as "out-group" difference, which further states how the "out-group" of China, constructed in the PAs before the transition, is transferred to be "in-group". This strategy is analysed in five aspects—title analysis, relations with China, positioning of HK, language policies, nationality issue and national education.*

Micro-strategies are strategies used to attach certain values to the "in-group" or "out-group". In other words, they are strategies to construct positiveness of the "in-group" and negativeness of the "out-group".

*References are studied on lexical level, including personal references, temporal references and spatial references.*
*Rhetorical devices are studied, including allusion and presupposition.*
*Intertextual strategy is analysed on intertextuality.*

This analytical framework attempts to bring the explanation and interpretation of the present data of the HK governments' PA in the discursive construction of HK identity. Specifically, the two chapters, Chapter 4 and Chapter 5, will be devoted respectively to this blueprint of investigation, analysis, description, interpretation, including the discursive strategies employed in the process of HK identity construction.

### 3.3.3 Analytical processes: the two processes in the discursive construction of an identity

Politicians who wish to influence public opinion, in this political discourse of PA to construct a HK identity for its people, however, have to contend with an opposing force: the general public's tendency, in accordance with Gricean pragmatics, to assume that a communicative act can be truthful or untruthful. Therefore, they have to be doubly strategic in their language use. They have to opt, on the one hand, for linguistic patterns which will imprint the desired view on the collective consciousness of a group and, on the other hand, they have to reduce the chances of dissent within this group by employing linguistic patterns which will back up their validity claim and curtail possible challenges to this claim. One way of achieving this is by using language that will positively represent the favoured worldview or the approved approach to a social, economic or global phenomenon as well as those who support this view or approach. The use of this language is usually accompanied by the use of its opposite, i. e., language which negatively depicts the opposing worldview or approach as well as those who hold these different opinions and values. Consequently, binary conceptualisations are very common in political communicative acts. They frequently take on the form of a polarisation between a legitimised insider group ( "us") and a delegitimised outsider group ( "them") . These binary conceptualisations serve a double purpose. First, the delegitimising of the outsider group aims to discredit possible challenges to the validity claim made by members of this group and simultaneously also attempts to strengthen the cohesion of the insider group. Second, the legitimising of the insider group aims to limit possible challenges to the validity claim by members of the in-group and thus, conversely, also seeks to weaken the cohesion of the outsider group. The repeated instantiation of these binary conceptualisations tends, furthermore, to lead to similar bipolar representations in the collective consciousness of the general public.

A wide range of linguistic means is at the disposal of the politician who wishes to influence public opinion through this use of binary conceptualisations. To achieve positive "self" or "us" presentation and negative "other" or "them" presentation, the politician can make a number of choices on the semantic, syntactic and lexical levels of language. For instance, a main semantic strategy, according to van Dijk (1997), "is to make propositions with positive predicates about the in-group rather explicit than implicit, rather direct than indirect, and stated rather than presupposed". The same semantic strategy is usually adopted for the supposed negative qualities of the out-group, which will also be made explicit and referred to directly. This semantic strategy is widely used in the PAs concerning what is addressed in the PAs and most prominently embodied in the construction of HK-China relations. Thus the discursive construction of the positive "in-group" presentation and the negative "out-group" presentation forms the basis of identity in discourse. But in this chapter, we are going to focus on the inter-sentential level of this strategy which starts with the labeling of social actors, proceeds to the generalization of negative attributions and then elaborate arguments to justify the exclusion of many and inclusion of some. Thus those who are positively constructed would be taken to be the "in-group" and those who are negatively constructed would be the "out-group". Furthermore, the negative side of the in-group and the positive side of the out-group will generally remain implicit, i. e. , unsaid, or will be referred to only indirectly and quite vaguely.

Therefore, HK identity is constructed in relation to other identities, marking those aspects that differentiate HK identity from the others. This way of difference should not be seen as the opposite of identity, but rather becomes one of the key aspects in the notion of identity (Woodward, 1997) . In this way identity clearly establishes the distinction between insiders and outsiders [to use Kramsch's (1998) terms]. As central to the idea of difference, and deriving from it, is that of the "other". Identity needs the "other" in order to define itself since it is the "other" who makes it possible to establish the differences. Oktar (2001) summarises, the development of social identity implies a two-step process: first, the identification and differentiation of two groups: "us" and "them"; and second, the attachment of certain values to each group which is of equal importance. Thus, as stated in Section 3.3, the two processes correspond to the two broad strategies in our analytical framework—macro-strategies and micro-strategies.

### 3.3.4 Theoretical approaches for interpretation and discussion

Based on the literature review in the previous chapter, it is evident that the present research is to be placed under the umbrella of CDA. The two major approaches in CDA—van Dijk's social-cognitive approach and Wodak's discourse-historical approach—are complementary rather than mutually exclusive. Thus a combination of these two approaches will be employed in doing the CDA in the present research which helps to bring a more critical and comprehensive and in-depth discourse analysis of the discursive construction of the HK identity in the present research.

In his social-cognitive approach, van Dijk (1995) essentially perceives discourse analysis as ideology analysis. According to van Dijk (1995), beliefs which are taken for granted and undisputed within a given culture are by definition not ideological within that culture (they may, of course, later or from another perspective be seen as ideological). In informal terms: ideologies presuppose competition, conflict, struggle, or differences of opinion and knowledge between groups. Ideologies are themselves constituted by basic propositions that represent what is good or bad for the group. They are, thus, based on the values and norms that each social group develops or borrows from more general cultural values (freedom, liberty, autonomy, truth, reliability, etc.). Discursive and experimental evidence suggests that ideologies tend to be polarised, e.g., as propositions about Us and Them, as is also suggested by the conflictual or competitive social basis of ideologies. Further, ideologies are organised by fixed ideological schema gradually learned and applied by social actors during their socialization and identification with various social groups. Categories in this schema are, e.g., membership criteria, typical actions, goals, norms and values, group position (relations with other groups), and specific group resources. These categories and their contents are some kind of group self-schema, defining the basics of their socio-cognitive identity. Thus, it can be concluded that discourses are mainly ideological and ideologies are mainly propositions about Us and Them—positive Us vs. negative Them.

With her discourse-historical approach, Wodak's approach, among other approaches in CDA, is the most linguistics-oriented and based on sociolinguistics. According to Wodak (1996):

*Discourse Sociolinguistics... is a sociolinguistics which not only is explicitly dedicated to the study of the text in context, but also accords both factors equal importance. It is an approach capable of identifying and describing the underlying mechanisms that contribute to those disorders in discourse which are embedded in a particular context—whether they be in the structure and function of the media, or in institutions such as a hospital or a school—and inevitably affect communication.*

According to Wodak & Ludwig (1999), language "manifests social processes and interaction" and "constitutes" those processes as well "discourse ... is always historical, that is, it is connected synchronically and diachronically with other communicative events which are happening at the same time or which have happened before". To Wodak, context is understood mainly historically (Meyer, 2001) and she distinguishes four levels of context: ① the immediate language- or text-internal co-text; ② the intertextual relationship between discourses; ③ the extralinguistic level which is called the "context of situation"; ④the broader socio-political and historical context. This discourse-historical approach finds its focal point in the field of politics, where it tries to develop conceptual frameworks for political discourse. Hence, it can be drawn that discourse is highly context-dependent.

Since the present research tends to be a critical one, theories from CDA will be drawn in our analysis of the discursive construction of HK identity, and a combination of van Dijk's social-cognitive approach and Wodak's discourse-historical approach will suit the research purpose of this study well and make the present research more revealing and critical.

## 3.4 A summary

Based on the theories in CDA and previous related studies, in this chapter we first raise our research question and labor a brief description of the data collected for the present research and research question. Then the analytical and theoretical frameworks are put forward, based on our case study in the research proposal. Lastly, related analytical theories are introduced in detail to be used in tacking the research questions. The following two chapters will probe in detail into the macro-and micro-strategies employed in the identity construction in the two HK governments' PA, with Chapter 4 elaborating an analysis of the macro-strategies and Chapter 5 an analysis of micro-strategies through which identities are constructed. These two chapters, Chapter 4 and Chapter 5, will reflect the two processes in the discursive construction of HK identities, and data in the research will be interpreted and discussed with the theoretical approaches from CDA as demonstrated in this chapter.

# Chapter 4 Macro Discursive Strategies in HK Identity Construction

## 4.1 Introduction

The previous chapter illustrated the overall design of this study and outlined the analytical framework employed to address the research questions at the macro-and micro-levels. This chapter tries to answer the question of what topics are involved in or excluded from the processes of the discursive construction of HK identity by analyzing such macro-strategies of content in the two sub-corpora of PAs.

Macro-strategies refer to the topics employed to establish a certain community identity by promoting intra-community sameness, similarity, unification, identification and solidarity, as well as the presupposition or emphasis of differences between differing societies. In this present research, we try to analyse the macro-strategies in two dimensions: firstly a content analysis of the three broad aspects of the PA's content, namely, cultural aspect, economic aspect and political aspect in the 22 PAs; secondly, an analysis of the topics that are addressed either in the PA before the transition or in the PA after the transition and that are prominently in contrast in the two sub-corpora of PA. It is also the macro-strategies that decide what to be included or excluded in the PA. Thus macro-strategies display what content should be involved in the Policy Address and how they contribute to the construction of in-group and out-group.

## 4.2 Content analysis

This section offers the results of an initial thematic analysis, which gives a first impression of what the two HK governments focused on in their PAs.

The logical starting point for analyzing texts is to consider the meaning of the text. All texts are about something (i. e. , they have content); and the most direct way of taking account of this is through content analysis. Developed by communication scholars in the early 20th century, content analysis was first used to measure the objective features (article length, size of headline, etc. ) of newspaper stories. During World War II, its scope was broadened to include various forms of propaganda including nonprint discourse. By the 1950s, content analysis had established itself in communication research as virtually synonymous with discourse analysis. Berelson's classic 1952 work defined it thusly: "Content analysis is a research technique that objectively, systematically, and quantitatively describes the manifest content of communication." (Berelson, 1952) . In recent decades, however, as discourse analysis itself has evolved into a broad variety of approaches ranging from ethnomethodology to artificial intelligence, content analysis has lost its status as the prime means of analyzing texts. Although in specific cases it can still serve that purpose, today it is more often used in a supporting role for more sophisticated forms of discourse analysis.

Content analysis has proved to be a useful foundational methodology. Here it might be defined as follows: Content analysis is the identifying, quantifying, and analyzing of specific words, phrases, concepts, or other observable semantic data in a text or body of texts with the aim of uncovering some underlying thematic or rhetorical pattern running through these texts (Berelson, 1952) . The key distinguishing characteristic to this approach is its focus on surface features (or "manifest content") . However, content analysis's emphasis on semantic or meaning-based patterns distinguishes it from more purely formal stylistic approaches such as register analysis (Biber & Finegan, 1994) or textlinguistic stylistics (Sandig, 1986) . Content analysis makes no claim to be a rich, definitive, or comprehensive method of analysis, as some critics have alleged. Given its limited scope, it cannot be so. Rather, content analysis typically serves to provide empirical grounding for other more sophisticated methods. It reflects the idea that it is possible to measure the content of texts by examining the statistic occurrence of defined units (such as arguments or phrases) . Therefore the first step in quantitative content analysis is to break down a text into countable units and work on statistical computations in relation to categories, defined by the analyst.

The unit that is worked with in the present research is the content categorization according to the headings, subheadings of the discourse as it is put by van Dijk (1991), topic can serve as an overview of the contents. Other studies like Peng's

(2005) study of China's multi-lateral diplomatic policies, which uses word counting and word percentage in the topic of multi-lateral diplomacy to show that the rise in word numbers and percentage in the government reports from 1986 to 2005 shows the government's reinforced attention to its multi-lateral diplomatic policies. Another study of Zheng (2006) also applies the rule that the higher percentage in the press conferences foregrounds the more importance of certain topics. Thus in the present research, we would like to break down the HK governments' PAs into several aspects—economy, culture and politics, all of which a government's PA is supposed to take into consideration, and which are to establish a certain identity by promoting intra-community sameness, similarity, unification, identification and solidarity, as well as the presupposition or emphasis of differences with other communities. And for these three aspects, word counting and its percentage in the PA will be analysed as an indication of the governments' different proportion of attention.

### 4.2.1 Three broad aspects in the PAs

We divide each PA into three very broad aspects of economy, culture and politics according to the headings of the sections in the PAs. When the headings do not reflect their contents, like the title of the second section in 1995 PA "The First Three Years", we have to scrutinize the content of the whole section to ensure which aspect of the three this section should belong to. Furthermore, when one heading belongs to a certain section in one PA and another section in another PA, we should make a decision of which category this heading belongs to and stick to it. Take the topic of "Crime" for example. It in some cases appears in the section of social life which is considered to be the cultural aspect but sometimes constitutes "Law, Order and Justice" which in this study contributes to the construction of common politics. Thus we should withdraw it from the original section and incorporate it into the aspect it is supposed to belong to. "Crime" should go more in agreement with "Law, Order and Justice" than with "social life".

In each PA, the two parts of introduction and conclusion are excluded from this content analysis because they are regarded as the comprehensive description or general abstract of the PA and cover nearly every aspect of our analysis of the PA and there are no clear-cut lines among the three aspects. If they were included, it would be very difficult to judge a particular sentence or paragraph contributing to a certain aspect. Thus the total word number may vary from that mentioned in the previous chapter.

In this way of calculation, the figures are rough but could show the tendencies in the PAs. The more words or the more proportion of words contribute to a certain aspect, the more attention or focus the government pays to this aspect, as stated in Peng (2005) and Zheng (2006).

#### 4.2.1.1 Common economy

Economy [according to Oxford English Dictionary (OED)], in economics, is defined as the human activity that consists in producing, exchanging, distributing, and consuming goods and services, as realized in an economic system. This aspect of common economy constructed in the HK governments' PAs is to cover a series of topics on finance, trade, industry, real estate market, business, exchanges, investment, etc., which are considered to be directly linked to the economic development or problems in HK. Table 3 shows the proportion of words devoted to the field of economy in each PA.

The figures in Table 3 concerning the construction of common economy roughly show that the British Colonial HK Government contributes less than the HKSAR Government in the discursive construction of common economy in their PAs. Especially in 1996PA, there is only one sub-heading among a total of 21 sub-headings in the whole PA, on the aspect of economy—Business as Usual. It is because 1996 was the last year of British colonial administration, and there were hardly eight months before the British withdrawal from HK in 1997, so to speak, the government had no longer term plan on the development of economy.

**Table 3 The number of words contributing to economy in the 22 Policy Addresses**

| Pre-transition | | | Post-transition | | |
|---|---|---|---|---|---|
| Year of PA | Words | Percentage (%) | Year of PA | Words | Percentage (%) |
| 1986 | 1 776 | 15.6 | 1997 | 2 815 | 18.7 |
| 1987 | 2 206 | 14.0 | 1998 | 5 006 | 27.5 |
| 1988 | 3 168 | 18.9 | 1999 | 1 523 | 8.0 |
| 1989 | 1 193 | 10.0 | 2000 | 1 537 | 10.9 |
| 1990 | 1 453 | 12.4 | 2001 | 2 014 | 15.6 |
| 1991 | 1 607 | 21.3 | 2003 | 6 481 | 83.1 |

(Continue)

| Pre-transition | | | Post-transition | | |
|---|---|---|---|---|---|
| Year of PA | Words | Percentage (%) | Year of PA | Words | Percentage (%) |
| 1992 | 2 603 | 17.6 | 2004 | 4 261 | 49.6 |
| 1993 | 1 086 | 6.0 | 2005 | 4 223 | 36.7 |
| 1994 | 1 267 | 10.6 | 2006 | 2 588 | 28.8 |
| 1995 | 3 614 | 20.0 | 2007 | 2 900 | 19.4 |
| 1996 | 329 | 2.9 | 2008 | 3 169 | 25.8 |
| Total | 20 302 | 13.6 | Total | 36 517 | 25.5 |

In 2003PA and 2004PA respectively, this aspect of economy is constructed with more than 80% and nearly half of the length of the whole PA, which is an extremely high portion. It is because in the year 2003 HK went through a lot of economic hardships in the Asian Financial Turmoil and also the infectious disease of SARS and the economy in HK was deteriorating.

Thus, we can see that in a PA, the government, with a certain proportion of length in the PA, tries to construct a common economic state for its people, be it a future plan or difficult situation. Further, the higher the proportion, the more concern is dedicated to this aspect. The HKSAR Government devotes more concern to the construction of common economy of HK than the British Colonial HK Government.

#### 4.2.1.2 Common culture

The United Nations Educational, Scientific and Cultural Organization (Unesco) (2002) described culture as follows: "... culture should be regarded as the set of distinctive spiritual, material, intellectual and emotional features of society or a social group, and that it encompasses, in addition to art and literature, lifestyles, ways of living together, value systems, traditions and beliefs" (according to OED). Thus, culture has a broad sense and can cover the whole range of social life. The aspect of common culture in the HK governments' PAs covers a broad variety of topics. The topics that belong neither to economy nor to politics are included in this aspect, varying from education, welfare, education, traffic, culture and recreation to infrastructure, tourism, etc. Table 4 shows the proportions of words devoted to the aspect of culture in each PA.

**Table 4 The number of words contributing to culture in the 22 Policy Addresses**

| Pre-transition | | | Post-transition | | |
|---|---|---|---|---|---|
| Year of PA | Words | Percentage (%) | Year of PA | Words | Percentage (%) |
| 1986 | 6 081 | 53. 5 | 1997 | 7 996 | 53. 2 |
| 1987 | 8 963 | 57. 0 | 1998 | 7 182 | 39. 5 |
| 1988 | 8 039 | 48. 1 | 1999 | 11 243 | 59. 5 |
| 1989 | 5 536 | 46. 8 | 2000 | 7 194 | 51. 2 |
| 1990 | 5 297 | 45. 2 | 2001 | 7 715 | 59. 8 |
| 1991 | 1 637 | 21. 7 | 2003 | 0 | 0 |
| 1992 | 5 132 | 33. 6 | 2004 | 1 680 | 19. 5 |
| 1993 | 7 824 | 43. 3 | 2005 | 4 267 | 37. 1 |
| 1994 | 3 747 | 31. 4 | 2006 | 3 517 | 39. 2 |
| 1995 | 9 123 | 50. 5 | 2007 | 6 879 | 46. 2 |
| 1996 | 0 | 0 | 2008 | 5 401 | 44. 0 |
| Total | 61 379 | 41. 1 | Total | 63 074 | 44. 1 |

First inspection of this group of figures shows no significant difference in the total proportion (41. 1% and 44. 1% respectively) that is devoted to the construction of common culture. Thus details should be investigated.

For one more time besides the aspect of common economy, the two PAs of 1996 and 2003 reveal their uniqueness of contributing no particular section to the construction of common culture. 1996—1997 is the last year of the colonial sovereignty, as indicated in the beginning of this PA by Christopher Patten, the "1995 Policy Address would be the last that I would give in the conventional form and manner" . While in 2003PA, it is essential for the government to dictate their overwhelming concern for other aspects except economy because only in which could the HKSAR Government find lawful shelter from being criticized for the explosion of the infectious disease, SARS and the thorny legislation of Article 23 in the BL.

Take two PAs of the highest proportion on culture aspect from the two groups—1986PA (53. 5%), 1987PA (57. 0%), 1999PA (59. 5%) and 2001PA (59. 8%) for comparison.

The topics contributing to this aspect in 1986PA are as follows:

*Education*

*Health and social programmes (including medical services, social welfare, labour, environment, broadcasting, control of obscene publication)*

*Development of infrastructure (including pubic works programme, housing, new towns, land development corporation, transport, communications, energy)*

Topics in 1987PA:

*Infrastructure (including transport, housing, urban development, environment)*

*Education*

*Health and social programmes*

*Culture and recreation*

*Travel and tourism*

Topics in 1999PA:

*Cultivating talents for a knowledge-based society (education)*

*Making Hong Kong an ideal home (environment)*

Topics in 2001PA:

*Government's role (in education, infrastructure, environment, relief measures)*

*Social policies (for family, young people, women and the elderly)*

In such a comparison of the topics that the PAs cover, it is evident that the previous two cover a far more variety of the topics than the last two though the previous two spend absolutely fewer words and less proportion of length on this aspect of culture. What is worth our particular attention here is the words applied as the headings in 1999PA. It dedicates 11 243 words to the two sections of "cultivating talents for a knowledge-based society" and "making Hong Kong an ideal home" which in straightforward ways should be sections of "education" and "environment". As the government's PA is delivered once a year, every facet of social life should be taken into account. Consequently it is believed that the HKSAR Government is getting into too much details of the same topics while ignoring some other fields.

#### 4.2.1.3 Common politics

Politics (according to OED), simply put, is the process in which groups of people make decisions. Politics is observed in all human interactions or social relations involving authority or power and refers to the regulation of a political unit, and to the methods and tactics used to formulate and apply policy. The aspect of common politics in the HK governments PAs covers some invariable topics like law, public service, governance, international relations which construct the common political situation for the HK people. Results of this aspect are shown in Table 5.

**Table 5 The number of words contributing to politics in the 22 Policy Addresses**

| Pre-transition | | | Post-transition | | |
|---|---|---|---|---|---|
| Year of PA | Words | Percentage (%) | Year of PA | Words | Percentage (%) |
| 1986 | 2 694 | 23. 7 | 1997 | 1 985 | 13. 2 |
| 1987 | 3 828 | 24. 3 | 1998 | 2 391 | 13. 1 |
| 1988 | 4 421 | 26. 5 | 1999 | 2 667 | 14. 1 |
| 1989 | 3 814 | 32. 2 | 2000 | 2 968 | 21. 1 |
| 1990 | 3 322 | 28. 4 | 2001 | 1 499 | 11. 6 |
| 1991 | 3 263 | 43. 4 | 2003 | 293 | 3. 7 |
| 1992 | 5 495 | 36. 0 | 2004 | 1 789 | 20. 8 |
| 1993 | 6 611 | 36. 6 | 2005 | 1 403 | 12. 2 |
| 1994 | 5 401 | 45. 2 | 2006 | 368 | 4. 1 |
| 1995 | 3 604 | 19. 9 | 2007 | 2 414 | 16. 2 |
| 1996 | 7 097 | 64. 0 | 2008 | 5 401 | 44. 0 |
| Total | 45 550 | 30. 5 | Total | 23 178 | 12. 7 |

Table 5 shows the proportions of words devoted to the aspect of common politics of HK. It seems that in this aspect of politics construction the two governments' PA differ to quite a large extent. First of all, the proportion of this aspect in the two groups of PAs vary a lot, with the proportion of the first group 30. 5%, more than double that of the proportion of the second group 12. 7%. The figures here show that the British colonial government show more concern for politics, as will be discussed in the later section. Secondly, the distribution of this aspect in a PA in these two groups varies to a vast degree. In the first group it can be seen that the different topics of the aspect of politics scatter in different sections of a PA, while in the second group, its distribution seems centralized in one or two sections.

From the above figures we can see that the PA with the highest proportion contributing to this aspect is 1996PA with 64.0%, and the PA with the lowest proportion, 1995PA with 19.9%, is still higher in proportion and more in absolute number of words than most of the PAs, nine in eleven, after the transition. As is mentioned above the British colonial government invested a lot of attention to politics in the PAs. We can see the following words in the beginning of 1996PA by Christopher Patten:

*... the handover of sovereign responsibility in Hong Kong from Britain to China, dictate another approach and impose other requirements... (the purpose of this Policy Address) To set out for you my own view of the great future that is open to Hong Kong in the years ahead; to explain how we have tried to lay the best possible foundations for that future; and to suggest what needs to be done over the coming years to make sure that Hong Kong moves on to even greater success (paragraph 1).*

In this particular PA, 16 out of the 20 topics go to the construction of common politics, another one goes to the aspect of economy and the rest 3 (A five-year agenda, Hong Kong's success story, and The rise of our city) are conducted to the overall situation in Hong Kong. Thereby we can equate politics, occupying 64.0% of the PA, with Patten's purpose of this PA. In other words, the construction of common politics is his goal in the PA.

The PA with the least proportion in the first group is the 1995PA, of which we should turn to the social background for explanation. In this year, outcomes of some of Patten's reform proposals made their appearance. The passage of his electoral bill—lowering the voting age from 21 to 18, adopting the "single-seat, single-vote" system for all elections, abolishing appointed members from the district boards and municipal councils—led to the Sept. 17th, 1995 Legco election in which Democrats confirmed their 91% victory and won two thirds of the seats, though previously Beijing announced that the Legco would be dissolved on the day of the handover. It can be inferred that in 1995PA Patten proposed little political reform in his PA.

The PA with the highest proportion in the post-transitional sub-corpus is delivered in the year 2000, and that with the lowest proportion in the year 2003. On June 29th, 2000, Hong Kong's middle class launched a protest urging the government to reform policies (International Herald Tribune, June 29th, 2000). Correspondingly, in this year's PA, we have such topics contributing to politics like Municipal Services-Reorganised for Efficiency, Civil Service Reform-Cautiously on Course. Coincidentally on July 1st, 2003, a massive demonstration went on to oppose the government's proposal to revise Article 23 and the Chief Executive, Dong's temporary shelving of the proposal, which might directly lead to the only section dedicating to politics in this year's PA—Legislating on Article 23 for the Basic Law. Therefore, it is reflected that the content of discourse helps the construction of social reality and the reality is constructive of political discourse.

### 4.2.2 A summary of the content analysis

From the above figures and tables on the construction of the three aspects in PA—economy, culture, and politics, we can have a glimpse of the inclinations of the two HK governments, the British colonial and the HKSAR.

The British Colonial HK Government dedicates much more to the construction of common politics and even takes it as its purpose in the PAs.

The HKSAR Government contributes more on the aspect of economy than the British Colonial Government because the enhancement of one aspect undoubted results in the decrease of another aspect.

Though the space on the aspect of common culture in the PAs of the two governments account for nearly the same proportion, after careful examination of the themes in this aspect, still discrepancies can be found that massive coverage of topics in the British Colonial HK Government's PAs contrasts with those in the HKSAR Government's.

From the PAs we can see the silhouette of what has happened, is happening and will happen in the community which redounds to the discursive construction of what the people in this community have experienced, be it achievement or hardship. The commonness of experience in economy, culture and politics in turn integrates the people into one identity of HK people.

Though the two sub-corpora vary to some extent as far as the content of the PA is concerned, the conclusion can be drawn that through the commonness in economy, culture and politics, intra-HK sameness and uniqueness are constructed (Wang, 2013).

After such a rough content analysis, what we have gained is only some very abstract tendency in the PAs of the two HK governments but that has become the foundational grounding for further analysis of the PAs. If we want to explore what are exactly included in or excluded from the PAs, the research should be complemented by the following topic analysis which directs to the specific topics in the PAs.

## 4.3 Topic analysis

Internal relations between the units and the textual whole are precluded from analysis and therefore quantitative content analysis runs the risk to neglect what might be important aspects of the textual meaning (Larsen, 1997; Asp, 1986; Fühlau, 1982). Thus, a complementing qualitative analysis of the overview of the contents—topic in the PAs—need to be provided.

Stemming from the critique of quantitative content analysis and hand in hand with a general rise against positivism, many Scandinavian media researchers subscribed to qualitative content analysis from an ideological perspective. This so-called "humanistic trend" in Scandinavian mass communication research started in the early 1970's. Much of the work focused on power relations moved towards qualitative analytical designs, often derived from the advances made in general and textual semiotics. Peter Larsen, one of the leading figures in qualitative content analysis in Denmark, described this trend as follows:

*Content analysis was, on the other hand, not considered to be an end in itself. Another characteristic feature of these studies, and another indication of the researcher's background in the humanities, was the "holistic" ambition, the attempt at interpreting media messages against broader historical, social and cultural contexts. To this should be added that the studies were usually grounded in a critical knowledge interest in emancipation (Larsen,* 1991).

According to Mayring (1983) qualitative content analysis is based on careful examination of the sources of the material to be analysed and on explicit observation and presentation of the analysts' own pre-understanding. Furthermore, qualitative content analysis has to take the perspectives of others into consideration and it has to be open towards re-interpretations. Semiotic terms, pragmatic theory of meaning and rules for interpretation from structuralist textual analysis are instruments in the analytical process, which includes the basic principles of summarising, explaining and structuring of the material (Mayring, 1983). This present research is done under the umbrella of CDA, thus, we adopt a CDA approach to explain, interpret our present data of the HK governments' PA.

As van Dijk puts it, the topics of discourse play a fundamental role in communication and interaction for discursive, cognitive and social reasons. Defined as "semantic macrostructures" derived from the local (micro) structures of meaning, topics represent what a discourse is about globally speaking, and embody the most important information of a discourse (van Dijk, 1980). They are the global meaning that language users constitute in discourse production and comprehension, and the "gist" that is best recalled by them. Hence the social relevance of topics in discourse in interaction and social structure: they define what speakers, writers orient towards and that has the most impact on further discourse and action. And topics, according to van Dijk & Kintsh (1983), are often expressed in discourse through titles, headlines, summaries etc., and they essentially define the situation (van Dijk, 1991). Because the important role topics have, topical analysis can be applied to larger corpora because an overall idea of what the discourse is about provides us other aspects of discourse and its analysis.

In this present research HK identity is defined as whether what embodied in the PAs identifies with the interests, values, beliefs and practices of Mainland China. Therefore we would proceed to an analysis of the topicalization in the PAs, focusing mostly on some topics that are significant in relation to China and some topics that are salient in one sub-corpus but obscured in the other. We'll first have a general analysis on the titles of the two sub-corpora in 4.3.1, and a comparison of the corresponding parts of "relations with China" in the two sub-corpora in 4.3.2, followed by a topic analysis of "nationality" in the pre-transition sub-corpus in 4.3.3 and "national education" in the post-transition sub-corpus in 4.3.4.

### 4.3.1 Titles of the Policy Addresses

Titles have important textual and cognitive functions and serve as the most conspicuous part of a news report—they are brief, printed on top or the first page, in large bold type, and often across several columns. Their main function is to summarize the most important information, or to project the discourse's theme or the writer's goal. That is, they express its main "topic" (van Dijk, 1991). Grammatically, titles are often incomplete sentence since articles or auxiliary verbs may be deleted. Topics also have an important cognitive function: they are usually read first and the information expressed in the titles is strategically used by the reader during the process of

understanding in order to construct the overall meaning, or the main topics, of the rest of the text before the text itself is even read. Further, titles are also used to activate the relevant knowledge in the reader's memory. The information conveyed through titles is used by the reader as an overall organizing principle for the representation of the content in memory and signals the reader how to define the content.

Titles often have ideological implications. Since they express the most important information of a discourse, they may influence the readers in their reading and understanding process: they summarize what, according to the writer, is the most important aspect, and such a summary necessarily implies an opinion or a specific perspective. Thus, the writer of a discourse may "upgrade" or "downgrade" the main topic. In other words, titles are a subjective projection, which influences the interpretation made by the readers. Generally speaking, the information in the title is also the information that is best recalled by the reader. This means that titles have a particularly important function in influencing the use readers will make of this information on later occasion (Schwarts & Flammer, 1981; van Dijk & Kintsh, 1983). In this study, the readers of the PA may first be the members of the Legislative Council and then the ordinary HK people. Through the analysis of the titles of the PAs, it can be revealed what important information the governors of HK Governor or Chief Executives project in their PAs. Not all of the 22 PAs possess a title. We've got the following:

**Table 6 Titles of the 22 Policy Addresses**

| Pre-transition | | Post-transiton | |
|---|---|---|---|
| Year of PA | Title of PA | Year of PA | Title of PA |
| 1986 | | 1997 | |
| 1987 | | 1998 | |
| 1988 | | 1999 | Quality People Quality Home—Positioning Hong Kong for the 21st Century |
| 1989 | | 2000 | Serving the Community Sharing Common Goals |

(Continue)

| Pre-transition | | Post-transiton | |
|---|---|---|---|
| Year of PA | Title of PA | Year of PA | Title of PA |
| 1990 | | 2001 | Building on Our Strengths Investing in Our Future |
| 1991 | | 2003 | |
| 1992 | | 2004 | Seizing Opportunities for Development—Promoting People-Based Governance |
| 1993 | | 2005 | Working Together for Economic Development and Social Harmony |
| 1994 | Hong Kong: A Thousand Days and Beyond | 2006 | Proactive, Pragmatic, Always People First |
| 1995 | Hong Kong: Our Work Together | 2007 | A New Direction for Hong Kong |
| 1996 | Hong Kong: Transition | 2008 | Embracing New Challenges |

In the pre-transitional sub-corpus of PA, three titles are catching. The title of 1994PA indicates the common future is limited and short as only a thousand days and changes may occur after that. What the governor wanted to call forth is a sense of urgency in the members of the Legislative Council, which has a lot of bearings. While in 1995PA title, the words "Our" and "Together" signify commonness. 1996PA title suggests the transition in the coming year is the most important. After reading the title of this PA, the reader may be indoctrinated either with the idea that transition would make everything different or what we could have done before the transition. The three pre-transition PAs all start with "Hong Kong" which imply that we are in Hong Kong which is our uniqueness and sameness, thus constructs a HK identity. The fact that only the last three of the PAs are entitled is quite significant in that the Governor attached much importance to these three PAs.

Urgency and time limit never exist in the titles of the post-transitional sub-corpus of PAs. Rather what is to convey in this group is the sense of "sameness" and "commonness" in the future lying ahead. Take 1999PA for example. The Chief

Executive tried to get HK and HK people prepared for the coming next century, thus, common future seems unlimited and tried at the same time to integrate HK people together by the word "position" which is the power of discursive construction in a PA. Moreover, in the eight entitled PAs in the post-transitional sub-corpus, we could find a lot of words signifying "sameness" and "commonness":

*"Quality people" "Proactive" "Pragmatic" unifying people together and showing the common feature all the HK people share;*

*"Sharing" "Building" "Working Together" and "Embracing" indicating that the same action or same behaviour;*

*"Common Goals" "Our Strength" "a New Direction" and "Our Future" illustrating that HK people are the all and the one and have a shared future.*

Furthermore, in the titles not only "sameness" and "commonness" can be perceived but a tincture of the specific era. The year 1999 is the turn of the century, thus looking forward to a common new century. "Opportunities" in 2004PA implies the support the central government granted to the HKSAR Government, and "Challenges" in 2008PA can be visioned the worldwide financial tsunami. Seen diachronically, the Chief Executives established a common history through such words. The titles of sub-corpus also embody the HKSAR Government's administration concept—"People-Base" and "People First" governance.

After a brief analysis of the titles of the two groups of PA, it can be concluded that both the two sub-corpora's titles try to suggest commonness and sameness, while the pre-transitional sub-corpus of PA carries a time limit in their titles and the post-transitional sub-corpus of PA tries to establish a common history, common future and common actions.

### 4.3.2 Relations with China

An abundant of the sections in the two sub-corpora of PA share the same topics and headings, but not all of them bear the same weight of significance in this research. As our HK identity is defined as a kind of relationship or to be identifying with Mainland China, the most prominent topic in the PAs should be the relation with China. In this section we are to discover whether the governments' stance in the PAs is identifying with or distancing from Mainland China. In our data, the HK relationship with China is discussed mostly from two angles—economic relations and political relations with Mainland China.

#### 4. 3. 2. 1 Relations with China before the transition

The PAs of 1987, 1988, 1989, 1990, 1991, 1993, 1994, 1995 in the pre-transition sub-corpus all contribute a section to the heading of "Relation with China".

The relation with China in the economic field before the transition is often defined as co-operation, which continues to grow, and from which China benefits. As in 1987PA, "China has remained our largest trading partner", and "Chinese investment in Hong Kong continues to grow, as do the financial links between us", and 1989PA states "we can also continue to be of benefit to China" . Such expressions imply that HK has the equivalent position as China in the co-operation whose benefits are bi-direction. As in 1990PA, "it would be difficult to overstate the importance of our economic relationship with China" . The British Colonial Government generally labels the "the breadth and depth of our relationship" with China as "partnership".

Compared with the positive economy "partnership" with China, the political relationship is not as positive and the relation of co-operation and mutual understanding need to be built up and further developed. In 1987PA, "dialogue helps to promote a relationship of co-operation and mutual understanding which will benefit both sides" and also "We have continued to build up and develop contacts with China at all levels" imply that a relation with sufficient mutual understanding has not yet established and constructed. In 1988PA, visits to HK by Chinese leaders "enable Chinese leaders to see for themselves how Hong Kong works" and such contacts "are important in building greater understanding on both sides" . Such wording shows that the China side does not understand the HK's way. Equally, in 1990PA, the HK civil servants "can become more familiar with China and the way in which China operates" . Besides, in 1991PA "the need for closer consultation and cooperation with China will increase, and our working contacts with China are already changing for the better" and 1994PA "There have been successes, but much, much more remains to be done" indicate the relationship with China need be improved and furthered and mutual understanding should be enhanced.

Difference or distance is an important concept in the construction of identity, which shows the attitude or position of distancing from the other party. In 1989PA "Hong Kong is linked to China but, in another important sense, separate from it" directly expresses separation and "our community has recognised the importance of not becoming directly involved in China's often complicated domestic politics" denotes the attitude of distancing from Mainland China. In 1991PA, "Hong Kong has developed social and economic systems very different from those of China. This does not mean that after 1997 the Hong Kong way of doing things will have to be brought in line with the systems in Peking: Hong Kong's way of doing things, and our own systems, will continue" not only illustrates difference but emphasizes that such difference cannot be removed. In the same PA, "Our aim and expectation should be that the good sense and goodwill which have resolved differences between the two side", here the "differences" refers to the different opinions in the administration of HK.

Furthermore, uncertainty in the future that results in the lack of confidence in the relations with China is also illustrated in 1987PA "the people of Hong Kong have been watching with great interest the drafting process of the document (the Basic Law) which will form the framework for the Special Administrative Region and which will also influence the evolution of our own systems before then", and "To leave uncertainty about Hong Kong's laws, uncertainty about rights of residence and about travel documents, uncertainty about air services agreements and uncertainty about arrangements for the return of fugitive offenders will do nothing to inspire confidence in Hong Kong's future". In 1989PA, words like "what happened in China created increased concern about the arrangements for Hong Kong's future" and "We for our part have made it clear to the Chinese Government that action is needed to restore confidence in the arrangements for Hong Kong's future" further render the relationship with uncertainty and lack of confidence.

Besides uncertainty, blocks, hindrances and problems do exist in the pre-transition China-HK relations. In 1990PA, words like "there are still, inevitably, stresses and strains which can only be overcome by mutual effort and mutual understanding", "(the HK government) to dispel misunderstandings and to improve our working relationship with Peking" express hindrance and disputes indwelling the relations. Thus the PA continues with "So there is much to do, and a need to tackle it quickly, pragmatically and efficiently". In 1991PA, hindrance and cumbrance are revealed in expressions like "even the most difficult problems in our relationship with China can be overcome", "this will enable it to resolve those issues which are still outstanding between the two sides", and "we seem to have had so many disagreements with Peking over important issues which affect the future". When reporting in 1994PA the work with the Preliminary Working Committee (PWC) which is positioned in this PA as "an advisory body of the National People's Congress", the addresser "do not believe it would be right for Hong Kong civil servants to attend formal meetings of the Preliminary Working Committee or its sub-groups", which shows his hostility and opposition to the PWC.

Tension and opposition are also present in the pre-transition China-HK relationship. In 1990PA, the British Colonial Government takes precautions not to give "the Chinese Government a veto over decisions which are properly for the Hong Kong Government to take", which makes it stand in opposition to the Chinese Government. In 1991PA, it is stated that "relations between the two sides have not always been as smooth as we would have liked" and "we cannot assume that our way of doing things will immediately be appreciated in Peking". Such tension is even furthered in 1994PA with the possible consequences of the failure of the relationship in words like "What is clear is that failure to settle the outstanding issues before 1997 will compromise Hong Kong's future stability and prosperity" and "it is the people of Hong Kong who will pay for a failure to complete the Joint Liaison Group's agenda by 1997".

#### 4.3.2.2 Relations with China after the transition

The economic relations with China is not only described as co-operation or co-ordination, also the concept is conveyed—China is the basis for HK's economic success. The following several aspects are constructed in the post-transition China-HK relations.

Sameness between China and HK: 1997PA: Hong Kong and China share the same fundamental interests; emphasizing the "One Country" concept and implementing "Two Systems" protect the interests of China and Hong Kong. Such words try to establish the sameness or commonness in shared interests and call attention to the belonging of one country or one nation which surely originates the same group of people with sameness in identity.

Dependence of HK on China: 1997PA: Hong Kong's prosperity and stability are closely linked with those of the Mainland; 2000PA: Hong Kong has long benefited from the country's strong support. I still firmly believe that when China succeeds, Hong Kong will prosper; 2001PA: Hong Kong's future development hinges on the economic growth momentum in the Mainland; 2003PA: Staunch support from the Mainland and our global outlook have been crucial to our economic success. 2005PA: The implementation of CEPA (agreed on by the CPG) has brought immediate benefits to our economy. Such wording in the PAs signifies HK's dependence on Mainland China and China's support for HK which in turn becomes an attraction or a force for the integration into the Mainland.

Integration with China: 2000PA: Hong Kong's residents are mostly Chinese, who take pride in their nation; identification of Hong Kong people with our cultural and historical roots; 2001PA: Over the past two decades, Hong Kong and the PRD (Pearl River Delta) have complemented each other, and together developed into a highly productive economic region; 2007PA: to embrace the era of globalisation, Hong Kong must find a suitable niche in the development of our country; Our economic integration with the Mainland is an irreversible trend. With the words quoted above, we can see evidence of HK's identification with the national pride and values of the Mainland.

Responsibility to China: 2000PA: They (HK people) should stand up and strongly support the nation; 2007PA: Hong Kong must find a suitable niche in the development of our country; we must abide by the Chinese Constitution and the Basic Law, 2003PA: ... enable us to continue to give strong support to our country; 2008PA: We can further contribute to the Mainland's economic development, to continue to give strong support to our country. Because aligning themselves with this community, HK should shoulder the responsibility of being a part of China.

Reduction of disagreement (Measures taken not to affect the relations): 2004 (the methods for selecting the Chief Executive) would affect the implementation of the Basic Law, the relationship between the CPG and the Government. The sensitive problem of CE selection might cause disagreement or displeasure in the Mainland, thus HK would like to be careful on this point in order to keep smooth relationship with Mainland China.

In sum, from the above analysis of the HK-China relations before and after transition, it can be concluded that before transition, the British Colonial HK Government, in the construction of HK-China relations, focuses more on differences and distance, describes uncertain future relations and problems and tensions, thus alienating HK people from Mainland China, while the HKSAR Government tries to establish sameness in interests, dependence of HK on Mainland, integration into the larger community of China, its responsibility to China as a part, and also unwillingness to cause disagreement in this relation. It can be concluded that the HKSAR Government tries to align HK people with Chinese and China's interests.

### 4.3.3 The positioning of HK

With common sense knowledge we know that Hong Kong, be it in the sovereignty of Britain or China, is resided by the same group of people doing more or less the same business and its position in the world seems to remain unvaried. Whereas, the way the Government positions this place influences the position of the people. Kress (1989) gives the example of the political leader whose role is to give definition of a new community. It is the leader's role to produce texts which bring the community in a unified manner. Thus it is essential to locate how the government positions HK in order to define what identity the government renders its people.

In the pre-transition PAs, HK is unfolded in the PAs from three aspects: ① it is portrayed as an Asia-Pacific regional centre with the fastest growing economy in order to give prominence to its economic and financial achievements. As addressed in 1989PA, "we play an important role in building up trade within the region. Goods going through HK from one part of the region to another, not counting China, have grown by 45% in the past year". HK is endowed with a lot of advantages to be a region center—its location; good communication; an efficient and apolitical administration; an impartial system of justice; a well-educated and efficient workforce and other conveniences. What is further emphasized as the characteristic of HK's position is its being regional and even international as is stated in 1990PA "an international business center". A number of facts are used to support this point, like the establishment of the International Business Committee and the vast number of overseas companies based in HK. In this particular PA, it is also stated that the commercial and financial relationships should be expanded around the world and HK wishes to play an active role in international organizations to help shape the world; ② HK is referred to as a gateway to China. Among HK's international relationships, China is one of the important. 1989PA shows that HK plays a key role in foreign investment in China because many foreign companies choose HK as their base to invest in China as HK has the advantages of back-up services like "unrivalled expertise" to deal with "Chinese officials and enterprises". What is emphsised in this respect is the benefit HK brings to China and the world, as stated in "HK will continue to be the best means of access to it (China)" and "by playing an intermediary role, we can also continue to be of benefit to China"; ③ HK's international image is two-faceted—a producer of cheap, low quality goods and a bustling, modern city of successful entrepreneurs. Here the characteristic of being "international" can be detected. From these three aspects, the pre-transition PA positions HK as economically international and a gateway to China.

The post-transition sub-corpus also depicts HK as a world-class city as is set forth in 1999PA, "Hong Kong must position itself firmly and clearly in the global economy". It further illustrates that "HK should not only be a major Chinese city but could become the most cosmopolitan city in Asia, enjoying a status comparable to that of New York in North America and London in Europe", which implied that HK, at the time being, is only a Chinese city, but it is probable to develop into a cosmopolitan city in Asia. Hence, it is connoted that HK is world-class to-be. Though possessing many of the key features common to New York and London, HK lags behind other international world-class cities in respects like human capital and living environment. However, HK has a "unique advantage"—"we have the thriving Mainland next to us". Thus, being next to China becomes a unique advantage in HK's efforts to be a world-class city.

In the two corpora, HK is positioned as an economically international centre in the pre-transition PA, while it is targeted as a world-class city in the post-transition PA; in the pre-transition corpus, HK is positioned as a gateway to China from whose relationship, China benefits. While in the post-transition corpus, HK is a major Chinese city and China becomes the unique advantage in HK's development. Hereby, in the previous corpus, HK people become people in an international city, while in the latter, HK people are Chinese people living in a Chinese city which works to be an international one. Before the 1997 Transition, HK is emphasised on its worldness and internationalness, whereas after the transition, it is stressed on its Chineseness.

### 4.3.4 Language policies

People read the identity of others with whom they come into contact based on features of behaviour, among which language is particularly central. In other words, we read the identity onto other people whose language we hear and read. Community identity tends strongly to correlate with shared languages, or in Joseph's (2004) words, "group identities" are manifested primarily through shared languages. Thus it is a fitting point to call community identities as double-edged swords. On the one hand, they fulfill the positive function of giving people a sense of who they are, of belonging to a community, in the absence of which one can feel a sense of alienation. On the other hand, such sense of belonging is always constructed through difference from "others"—a categorical distancing that can all too easily turn into a desire for segregation. In the case of HK, English is the "controlling" official language before the 1997 Transition while after the transition, Chinese version of document is prevailing. In sum what languages the HK governments promote or stipulate the HK people speak is also the central point in the construction of HK identity.

Together with English and Chinese, another Chinese dialect, Cantonese, is the local HK language. What makes the case of HK linguistically intricate has partly to do with the use of English, but at least as much with what is covered by the word "Chinese". Although there is a relatively unified written Chinese that literate people throughout the Chinese-speaking world share, there is little mutual comprehensibility between Putonghua, the official spoken language in China, and other local dialects like Cantonese. Linguists like Joseph (2004) claim that the linguistic distance between Putonghua and Cantonese has been compared to that between English and Swedish.

In our present corpus of the HK governments' PA, five PAs are found to be concerned with language education and language promotion in HK.

In the year 1986, it is proposed in the PA that "it is intended that authentic Chinese versions of our laws should be enacted by this council" (p. 127, "p" henceforth stands for "paragraph"), which can be interpreted that the first time that written Chinese was to appear in official documents. The same PA continues with "the government is continuing to make provision for the wider use of Chinese in official business" in which the "Chinese" can only refer to the local HK spoken language of Cantonese. It can be inferred that in the year 1986 and years after that and before 1997, bilingualism of English and Cantonese exists orally in the workings of the HK government and bilingualism of English and Chinese versions of document prevails only in the field of laws.

The next PA which contributes to language promotion in HK is in the year 1997, the time immediately after the transition. In paragraph 84, it is claimed that "our goal for secondary school graduates to be proficient in writing English and Chinese and able to communicate confidently in Cantonese, English and Putonghua" and also "Putonghua will become part of the curriculum ... and a subject in the HK Certificate of Education Examinations by the year 2000". Such words indicate that HKSAR Government's dedication to the promotion of Putonghua in HK and also their determination to integrate the language in HK into that of Mainland. As has been stated above, language is a token of one's identity. It is evident the first day from the transition, the HKSAR Government is devoted to the promotion of Putonghua thus the promotion of a Chinese identity among the HK people.

1999PA declares that "it is the SAR Government's goal to train our people to be truly biliterate and trilingual... we have established language benchmarks for those teaching English and Putonghua" (p. 69) and that "mother-tongue teaching was introduced ... most secondary schools adopted mother-tongue teaching the both their cognitive and learning abilities". It is evident that along with the determination to promote spoken Chinese Putonghua in HK, HKSAR Government also takes some measures like the benchmarks to promote Putonghua in HK. HKSAR Government seems to focus more on the promotion of Chinese than anytime in history.

Situation turns a bit different in 2001PA (p. 46) which states "it is our policy to promote bi-literacy and tri-lingualism. Hong Kong is a cosmopolitan city, and it needs to promote the wider use of basic English. As part of China, Hong Kong people should also learn to speak fluent Putonghua." It is the first time after the transition that the importance of English is mentioned in the PA. The same PA continues with the discussion on the Native-speaking English Teacher Scheme (p. 47 ~ 48) and also "from the start of next school year, we will strengthen English language teaching". It seems that in this particular time, the HKSAR Government turns to the promotion of English in education and the emphasis is shifted to English as a global language in HK.

The last PA that shows concern for language education and promotion is in the year 2006 in which it states (p. 43) "the Standing Committee on Language Education and Research has also allocated funds to enhance the effectiveness of English language teaching... and to subsidise overseas training for teachers". Such words denote the sheer emphasis on the promotion of English on the part of the HKSAR Government without mentioning the importance of Chinese or Putonghua in HK.

Through the above analysis of the five PAs that contribute to language issues in HK, we can see an n-shape in the promotion of Chinese in HK throughout the span of 22 years of the PAs. In the two decades before the transition, English has been changing from being a purely colonial language whose use was largely restricted to government circles, the law, high-level business, and a few other sectors, to becoming an indispensable language of wider communication, for a growingly large range of people (Lord, 1987). While upon the transition, one of the first and the most powerful policies of the SAR administration was over language policy. The government's proposal that the language of instruction in government-run schools shifts from English to Cantonese met with vehement opposition form parents (Joseph, 2004) who contended that their children would be put at a disadvantage in their future careers by not being taught in English and who took to the streets in protest, until the government retreated to a compromise position to resume English as a teaching language (as can be seen in 2006PA).

HKSAR Government's eagerness to incorporate into Mainland China, especially demonstrated in setting the benchmarks for Putonghua, according to some sociolinguists (Joseph, 2004), is not supported by Beijing whose position on language in HK universities and education has been clear and consistent—it does not support making Putonghua the main teaching language. China is full of Putonghua-language universities, in the PRC's view, and it needs HK as its English-speaking bridge to the rest of the world.

The protest inside HK and the lack of support from the Beijing side lead to the resumption of English as a language of instruction in HK. Despite the fact that English has restored its status, Putonghua is still coming into use and gaining increasing importance in HK because of the benchmarks that HKSAR Government has set for it, which is also an indication of HKSAR Government's integration into Mainland China.

As a result we can see that language use in HK can be viewed as the outcome of several forces. Before Transition, forces at play were the British Government, the British Colonial HK Government, the HK people, and more implicitly, the Chinese Government (Wang & Ge, 2012a). As is known HK Governors before the transition were all British, which, to a great extent influenced the language use in HK. Whereas after transition, the three forces at play in determining the language use in this community are HKSAR Government and its mother government, the Central People's Government (CPG) and people in HK. In order to keep a balance between the CPG and HK people, the HKSAR Government has to minimize its voice or its intention in the PA—the promotion of Putonghua in education and the determination of integration into Mainland China.

### 4.3.5 Nationality issue and national education

Before the 1997 Transition, nationality was a prominent issue for HK people. Under the 1981 British Nationality Act, HK people, holders of BDTC (British Dependent Territories Citizen) passport, free to enter the UK without a visa, were for the first time in the past 150 years denied the right to settle in Britain. This Act was an abdication by the British Government to protect its own citizens, for which the HK people found themselves second-class citizens in Britain because even the Macau people had the right of abode in Britain as the holders of full Portuguese passport. The Hong Kong (British Nationality) Order 1986 provides that persons who are British Dependent Territories citizens, by virtue of a connection with Hong Kong, may apply for a British National (Overseas) passport before July 1st, 1997 which offers its holders to enter UK without a visa but no right of abode.

1986PA tries to reassure the HK people with the words like "identity card, for both permanent and temporary residents, will be available from July lst, 1987, and may continue to be used until they are replaced" and the passport "give Hong Kong residents confidence in their ability to travel freely in the transition period, and after 1997".

After some proposals, in April 1990, Britain finally introduced the British Nationalities (Hong Kong) Bill which offered 50 000 heads of household full British citizenship the right of abode in the UK to those whose skills and services were thought most vital to HK. This measure, stated in 1990PA, is still to deny most HK people right of abode in the UK and to guarantee that "the vast majority of people ... will stay here permanently" because the arrival of over 3 million people from HK would sharply increase Britain's "ethnic-minority population".

Therefore, it can be concluded that HK people were refused by the British Government and their status and identity were ambiguous, as is illuminated in 1995PA "It will be very hard for people to have confidence in Hong Kong if their own personal status is ambiguous. People need certainty about their residence rights, their travel documents and visa-free access to foreign countries" . Thereafter, before transition, HK people are ethnic Chinese but not Chinese citizens and are British citizens holding BNO passport but without full British citizenship.

Nationality has never been of concern in the post-transition PA because its historic significance ceases the moment transition occurs because HK people acquire their home-visiting certificates delivered by HKSAR Government.

Another topic worth of attention is "National education" which has not made its presence in the PA until 2007. It is understandable that the British Colonial Government would not promote "national education", but the HKSAR Government does not project this topic in the first ten years of transition. As Flowerdew (2002) puts it, the CE needed to maintain the confidence on the part of HK people that there would be little change from the old system. It is for this reason that the topic "national education" makes its debut in the PA only as late as 2007. It might have appeared earlier because Deng Xiaoping, previous Chinese leader, when addressing BLDC said, "HK's administrators should be people of HK who love the Motherland and HK". ("Speech at a meeting with the members of the committee for drafting the Basic Law of the HKSAR" in selected works of Deng Xiaoping (vol. 3). Beijing: Foreign Languages Press, pp. 214 ~ 220. (Flowerdew, 1998)

What leads the HKSAR Government to establish a policy to promote national education is: first, it is the government's duty to "help everyone to know more about our fast-developing motherland"; second, "a better understanding of our country" will enable HK people to have "a brighter future". As for the first reason, it is understandable that national education is the government's duty as is stated by Deng Xiaoping and also in 2007PA by Hu Jintao, the Chinese leader being, at the welcoming banquet HKSAR Government hosted on June 30th, 2007. However, it seems that "a better understanding of our country" has no direct relation to HK people's "brighter future". But in association of the previous parts in this chapter, there is no doubt that dependence on the Mainland and convergence into the development of the Mainland are beneficial to the HK development.

Moves taken to realize national education include lectures and training programmes, opportunities for HK students to join Mainland study trips, launching a National Education Funding Scheme, more weight added to the elements of national education in the existing primary and secondary curricula, schools forming flag guard teams and staging more national flag-raising ceremonies. Further, the 2008 Olympics was taken as an excellent opportunity to promote a shared sense of national pride. Such kind of moves and measures seem in line with the national education in Mainland China which shows not only an integration into Mainland but also the eagerness to conform to the practice in China which goes in line with the definition of identity in the present study—to identify with certain social groups and to align with the interests, values, beliefs and practices of these groups.

The topics of "nationality issue" and "national education" are only projected in either corpus of the pre-transition or post-transition. In the pre-transition PA, the topic of nationality issue tries to construct a sense of difference—HK people's difference from British people though they hold a BNO passport. While in the post-transition PA, the topic of national education constructs sameness, identifying with the interests and practices of Mainland.

These two topics in the PA also indicate that discourse is the contending field of multilateral forces (van Dijk, 1991) . Before the 1997 Transition, HK people worried about the future of HK and nationality issue became what they are concerned. The British Colonial HK Government had to keep a balance between the HK people and the British Government. However, after the Transition, HKSAR Government could not put forward their national education immediate after 1997, and not until 10 years after the transition did the Government proposes such a topic and a balance between difference forces is thus struck. Therefore, the HK-China relationship becomes the determinant element in such topics. And the acceptability of the HK public is also involved in the discourse.

### 4.3.6 A Summary of the topic analysis

In this section of topic analysis, we compare the titles of the PAs in the two sub-corpora and also the most prominent topics of relations with China, the positioning of HK, language policies, and nationality issue and national education. Firstly, in the pre-transition PAs, the urgency of time can be connoted while the post-transition PAs try to construct the continuity in history, culture and future. Secondly, on the topic of Chinese relationship, the pre-transition PAs tend to present differences, problems and even tensions, taking HK as a world city; while the post-transition PAs tend to show the advantages of incorporating into Mainland China, constructing HK to be one of the Chinese cities and HK people Chinese people. In the process of the identity shift, the policy of language contributes greatly in the promotion of Putonghua in HK education. Lastly, when addressing the nationality issue, the British Colonial Government tends to identify its HK people to the British Nationality overseas, while HKSAR Government preaches at the ethnic origin of its HK people and propagates its doctrine that HK people should love their motherland and ancestral country.

With these titles, headlines and topics, the pre-transitional sub-corpus tends to emphasize the differences, distance, and even tension or disputes between HK and China and thus constructs China as out-grouped to HK; while the post-transitional sub-corpus is inclined to construct China as in-grouped with HK by aligning HK's interest, values, language with China's and stressing the sameness of Chinese people and avoiding possible differences between HK and China.

## 4.4 A summary

In this chapter, we may conclude, from a very general content analysis of the two sub-corpora of PA before and after the transition, that the British Colonial HK Government focuses more on the construction of common HK politics in its PAs and HKSAR Government puts more emphasis on the construction of common HK economy in its PAs. Therefore, the strategy of constructing common HK politics is as important to the British Colonial Government as the strategy of constructing common HK economy to HKSAR Government. This general content analysis shows the construction of commonness and sameness that are shared by the HK people and unique to HK people, or in other words, intra-HK sameness.

From a following analysis of topicalization in the two sub-corpora of PAs, it is evident that besides constructing the sameness and commonness in HK, the two sub-corpora differ a lot in their topics. The topic analysis shows that more or less on the same issues, the British Colonial HK Government and the HKSAR Government construct different HK identities, the previous transient, international and aligning a bit with Britain and distancing from Mainland China, the latter lasting, Chinese, aligning with China and Chinese values or integration into China.

In conclusion, the macro discursive strategies are employed to construct commonness within HK and to construct the in-group and out-group of HK. Results show that both the two sub-corpora of PA apply the macro strategies to construct HK sameness and an out-grouped China in the pre-transitional PA and an in-grouped China in the post-transitional PA, which corresponds to the first analytical process of construction of in-group and out-group.

# Chapter 5 Micro Discursive Strategies in HK Identity Construction

## 5.1 Introduction

The previous chapter, the analysis of the macro-strategies in the discursive construction of HK identities, answered the question of what is addressed in the two sub-corpora of PA which constituted the first step in our analytical process, as in Oktar's (2001) words, the construction of sameness versus difference in and between the "in-group" and "out-group". While this chapter tries to look into the micro-strategies in an attempt to answer the question of how and what linguistic devices are employed, which forms the second step in our analytical process of the attachment of certain values to each group, in which "in-group" is always favourably described and "out-group" is associated with negative traits, or what was generally referred to as positive self-presentation in opposition to negative other-presentation. The discursive realizations can be more or less intensified or mitigated, more or less implicit or explicit, due to historical conventions, public levels of tolerance, political correctness, and the specific context and public sphere.

The micro-strategies are processed in three aspects—referential strategies which are lexical units existent on the level smaller than sentence, rhetorical strategies which are on the sentential level, and intertextual strategies which belong to the textual level. Thus in this chapter, the analysis of the discursive strategies at the three levels will be presented in three sections and followed by a summary in this chapter.

## 5.2 Referential strategies

*Deixis belongs within the domain of pragmatics because it directly concerns the relationship between the structure of language and the contexts in which they are used*

(*Levinson*, 1983).

The quotation above is unambiguously locating deixis as an aspect of meaning in use in context. Also called "indexicals" or "indexical expressions", deictics are linguistic pointers which orientate reference in an utterance to "the contextual coordinates of the utterance" (Mey, 2001). The situation of deixis therefore presupposes a speaker who provides meaning for an utterance, and expects the audience to interpret the utterance's meaning from the speaker's viewpoint. In more general terms, deictics to some degree can be used to mean references, but references most of the time are explicit and in Wodak's (1999) study, is a linguistic means in the discursive construction of national identity. Salience and mutual knowledge or givenness is the crucial aspect the speaker considers when he performs a referential act. In the current study, our attention has been focused primarily on lexical units of references which serve to construct unification, unity, sameness, difference, uniqueness, heteronomy and so on. The most important of these are: personal reference (deixis "we"), spatial reference (toponyms/geonyms), and temporal reference (nouns with temporal meaning, verb tense), which are considered to be the three sub-strategies of the referential micro-strategy on lexical level.

As linguistic operations or choices may be overt or covert in nature but Butt, et al (2004) claim that choices on lexical level of language tend to be more or less overt, in the sense that they rarely go fully unnoticed by the listener or reader since they lie above the threshold of consciousness. The frequency with which linguistic choices and patterns linked to a particular worldview are instantiated in a communicative act or series of acts may lead to their habituation. They become part, as Butt, et al. (2004) point out, not only of the meaning potential of a political actor or group of actors but also over time of the "general public's collective meaning potential". In other words, the repeated linguistic choices and discursive patterns influence the general public's conceptualisations. They play the role of establishing a common view of the world and lead to shared views of social, economic and global phenomena.

### 5.2.1 Personal reference

The first-person plural pronoun "we" is the most complex among all the pronouns and can well be used in the service of "linguistic imperialism" to verbally annex and usurp. As Volmert (1989) argues:

*A speaker has at his/her disposal a whole range of (clever) options with which to present the interests and affairs of "we-groups" in the public sphere. In a speech during an election campaign, for example, a speaker can unite himself and his audience into a single "community sharing a common destiny" by letting fall into oblivion all differences in origin, confession, class and lifestyle with a simple "we". This "community sharing a common destiny" may be bound by different degrees of intimacy and familiarity: from the common economic interests of "society as a whole" to the emotional needs of a family-type community (Volmert, 1989).*

Linguistic studies usually distinguish between an addressee-inclusive and addressee-exclusive "we", and between a speaker-inclusive and speaker-exclusive "we". The categorization remains rather vague. We refer to the possible categorization by Wodak (1999) as follow as the study of "we" takes into account the correspondent "our", "us" and "ours":

*Uses of "we"*

| | |
|---|---|
| *a. I + you* | *partially/totally addressee-inclusive* |
| *b. I + he/she* | *addressee-exclusive* |
| *c. I + you (plural)* | *partially/totally addressee-inclusive* |
| *d. I + they* | *addressee-exclusive* |
| *e. I + you + he/she* | *partially/totally addressee-inclusive + ?* |
| *f. I + you (plural) + he/she* | *partially/totally addressee-inclusive + ?* |
| *g. I + you (plural) + they* | *partially/totally addressee-inclusive + ?* |

In the present study, the addressee may be members of the Legislative Council because the PA is delivered by the Governor or the CE at the opening of the yearly session of the Legislative Council, or when it is publicized the Hong Kong people may be the addressee. In this communication event, the addresser may be the Governor or the CE in person or he may speak in the voice of his Government (as has been mentioned above, the Governor/Executive speaks for the Government). Wodak, et al. (1999) consider the repeated use of the pronoun "we" in political discourse a "persuasive linguistic device which helps invite identification and solidarity with the 'we-group', which, however, simultaneously implies distancing from and marginalization of 'others'." In sum, this present sub-referential strategy will be both qualitative and quantitative, in other words, not only the uses of "we" is analysed but also the times of its presence.

Thus we categorize the references of "we" (including "our" "ours" and "us") from the narrowest meaning "the Hong Kong Government" to a blurred meaning "the Hong Kong Government and Hong Kong People" to the broadest "Hong Kong and China" as follows:

| | |
|---|---|
| "*we* 1" | *the Governor/ the CE + the LC - the HK Government* |
| "*we* 2" | *the HK Government + the HK People - HK* |
| "*we* 3" | *HK + China* |

Thus "we" is used to invite identification and solidarity in certain group of people and those that are excluded are distanced and marginalized as out-grouped. Some examples of the uses of "we" are offered.

"*we* 1": *We will carry out a programme...*
*Our schedule...*
"*we* 2": *...what all this meant for our lives...*
*Our economy; our society;*
*We have being going through...*
"*we* 3": *our country*

But not always is the "we" used so clear-cut. For example, the "we" in "our police complaints" may be blurred, but the present author considers that "police" belongs to the whole community and should be grouped in "we 2".

Table 6 presents the use of "we" in the pre-transition sub-corpus. 1986PA shows a low percentage of use of "we" which in our previous case study agreed with Flowerdew's (2004a) that the Governors, as foreigners to HK seldom used the inclusive "we". However, the systematic analysis of the 11 years of PA shows that the HK Governors tended to use 25 "wes" per 1 000 words in the PAs, with 986PA an exception.

**Table 7 The use of the personal reference of "we" in the pre-transitional PA**

| PA | We 1 | | We 2 | | We 3 | | Total | |
|---|---|---|---|---|---|---|---|---|
| | TOP* | Perc. (%) | TOP | Perc. (%) | TOP | Perc. (%) | TOP | Per 1 000 words |
| 1986 | 14 | 17.2 | 67 | 82.8 | 0 | 0 | 81 | 7.1 |
| 1987 | 83 | 28.0 | 213 | 72.0 | 0 | 0 | 296 | 18.8 |
| 1988 | 70 | 19.3 | 292 | 80.7 | 0 | 0 | 362 | 21.7 |
| 1989 | 83 | 21.3 | 305 | 78.7 | 0 | 0 | 388 | 32.8 |
| 1990 | 56 | 17.0 | 273 | 83.0 | 0 | 0 | 329 | 28.1 |
| 1991 | 49 | 25.9 | 140 | 74.1 | 0 | 0 | 189 | 25.1 |
| 1992 | 105 | 26.6 | 289 | 73.4 | 0 | 0 | 394 | 25.8 |
| 1993 | 108 | 20.6 | 395 | 79.4 | 0 | 0 | 523 | 29.5 |
| 1994 | 96 | 23.8 | 307 | 76.2 | 0 | 0 | 403 | 33.8 |
| 1995 | 103 | 17.7 | 479 | 82.3 | 0 | 0 | 582 | 32.3 |
| 1996 | 112 | 35.3 | 205 | 64.7 | 0 | 0 | 317 | 28.6 |
| Total | 979 | 25.3 | 2 965 | 74.7 | 0 | 0 | 3 864 | 25.9 |

* TOP stands for "time of presence"; Perc. stands for "Percentage".

The following is another table indicating the use of "we" in the pre-transition sub-corpus.

**Table 8 The use of the personal reference of "we" in the post-transitional PA**

| PA | We 1 | | We 2 | | We 3 | | Total | |
|---|---|---|---|---|---|---|---|---|
| | TOP | Perc. (%) | TOP | Perc. (%) | TOP | Perc. (%) | TOP | Per 1 000 words |
| 1997 | 93 | 18.0 | 411 | 79.9 | 10 | 2.1 | 514 | 34.2 |
| 1998 | 125 | 17.7 | 570 | 81.0 | 8 | 1.3 | 703 | 38.6 |
| 1999 | 89 | 16.3 | 440 | 80.5 | 17 | 3.2 | 546 | 28.9 |
| 2000 | 85 | 20.0 | 324 | 76.9 | 12 | 3.1 | 421 | 30.0 |
| 2001 | 73 | 17.8 | 330 | 80.4 | 7 | 1.8 | 410 | 31.8 |
| 2003 | 54 | 16.9 | 261 | 81.8 | 4 | 1.3 | 319 | 40.9 |

(Continue)

| PA | We 1 | | We 2 | | We 3 | | Total | |
|---|---|---|---|---|---|---|---|---|
| | TOP | Perc. (%) | TOP | Perc. (%) | TOP | Perc. (%) | TOP | Per 1 000 words |
| 2004 | 53 | 16. 4 | 265 | 82. 0 | 5 | 1. 6 | 323 | 37. 6 |
| 2005 | 76 | 19. 6 | 302 | 78. 0 | 9 | 2. 4 | 387 | 33. 6 |
| 2006 | 65 | 27. 7 | 157 | 67. 0 | 12 | 5. 1 | 234 | 26. 7 |
| 2007 | 54 | 13. 7 | 301 | 76. 4 | 39 | 9. 9 | 394 | 26. 5 |
| 2008 | 63 | 19. 7 | 238 | 74. 6 | 18 | 5. 9 | 319 | 26. 0 |
| Total | 830 | 18. 2 | 3 599 | 78. 7 | 141 | 3. 1 | 4 570 | 32. 0 |

In the above figures, we found no significant difference in the times of the use of "we" in the two sub-corpora which might be very different from Flowerdew's (2004a) study stating that the last HK Governor used much fewer "we" than the first HK CE due to the fact that the Governor is a foreigner to HK. Flowerdew further claims that the first HK CE used more inclusive "we" because he is a Hongkonger. Because Flowerdew studies only the first four or five years of the CE's speeches, from which we can also detect a sharp change in the times of presence of "we" in the PAs, the CE may try to make adaptation to his speech in the later years of his post. Another reason for the different discovery of the present study may lie in the different data of study. The data in Flowerdew's study include a lot of oral speeches or interviews while the present study is solely restrained to the highly institutionalized genre of PA which is expected to display less sharp difference. Flowerdew's explanation that the Governor being a foreigner influences his use of inclusive "we" seems not significant at all in this study of PA, because in the latter years after the transition, the HK CE tends to use fewer "we", especially in the years 2006, 2007, 2008, the use of "we" seems to conform to its use in the pre-transitional sub-corpus in its proportion and also times of presence.

From the above two tables, it is evidently significant that every PA varies in their use of "we 1" "we 2" and "we 3". Difference can be detected that pre-transition corpus applies no "we 3" though the proportion of "we 3" in the post-transition corpus is still low. But vast significance lies in this yes-no distinction. As is captured by Wilson (1990) the distinction of different groups is dependent on the speaker's perception of the use of personal indexicals. If the speaker perceives "those" as more negative, with "those" associated with facelessness, then "those" will be placed further away from "we". As such, it is the speaker's intention and attitude to the topic of discussion that condition his/her use of the personal reference "we". In conclusion, pre-transition PA corpus distances China from the HK in-group, while the post-transition corpus places China in-grouped with HK through repeated use of this personal reference of "we", as is claimed by Wang & He (2012b).

To conclude, the use of "we" is a significant and important lexical strategy in the construction of "in-group" and thus words with positive connotations will be used to describe the in-group and its qualities whereas those that are excluded from the in-group must be linked with negative connotations to evoke negative feelings towards the out-group. As Wodak, et al. (1999) put it, the repeated use of the pronoun "we" in political discourse a "persuasive linguistic device which help[s] invite identification and solidarity with the 'we-group', which, however, simultaneously implies distancing from and marginalization of 'others'".

### 5.2.2 Temporal references

These temporal references, together with verb tenses and lexical choices with semantic components indicating "succession" and "progression" are strategies of continuation (Wodak, et al., 1999) which help construct a cohesive community identity. Temporal references concern the "when" of the utterance. The time of an utterance is reflected by the verb-tense (past present future) and adverbs of time (e.g, then, now). Therefore this type of references is divided into three temporal categories or tenses of "past" (before the moment of utterance), "present" (at the moment of utterance) and "future" (after the moment of utterance).

As tense is used to construct the past, the present and the future thus a powerful strategy in constructing the commonness and uniqueness that people possess of their future or history. People cannot break down history so the transferred sovereignty still brings the past to the present and the present to the past. Here we are to look into the two tenses, past tense which contributes to the construction of a common past history and future tense which constructs a common future, in the texts. In studying tense, temporal reference is most significant (Wodak, 1999) including temporal prepositions, adverbs of time and adverbial constructions.

#### 5.2.2.1 Temporal references indicating the past

As is analysed above, temporal references indicating the past is to construct a common history. In the pre-transitional sub-corpus, this lexical strategy is used to construct the achievements of the British Colonial administration in HK and without referring to HK's history before the occupation of Britain, which is embodied in the present examples:

—*GDP has grown by* 18 *per cent in real terms to US* $ 23 800 *per head.*
—*New investment has grown by* 31 *per cent in real terms.*
—*Total visible exports have grown by* 43 *per cent in real terms, and total exports of services have grown by* 31 *per cent.*
—*Our fiscal reserves have grown by* 57 *per cent, to total* $ 151 *billion.*
—*Tax rates have been cut to provide reductions for almost every salaried employee.*
— *And, of course, the share of public spending has remained firmly below* 20 *per cent of GDP.* (1995*PA*, *p.* 8)

These examples of past temporal references focus on the achievements of HK which confirm the principle that self-representation is always positive. While another example of past temporal references may not be totally in the same case as follows:

*The first half of* 1986 *was marked by a strong recovery in Hong Kong's domestic exports which have grown by* 8% *in real terms since the same period last. Domestic exports and re-exports to China continued to be affected by the tighter control on imports which were adopted by China in early* 1985. (1986*PA*, *p.* 14)

With the use of the past tense and the temporal reference of "the first half of 1986" readers are informed of the increase in exports which are achieved supposedly through the joint efforts of the government and the people. The second half of this example also implies that exports of HK do not depend on China because exports grow drastically with the tighter control on China's imports thus indicating China's negative effect on HK's economy.

This same strategy is also employed in the post-transitional corpus, but since the history after the transition seem comparatively short, this strategy is mainly used to mention the short-term achievements of HK and also benefits from China. The CE seems to devalue the period before transition with some negative words or words with negative connotations in constructing the Colonial Government or the colonial period. Examples are as follows:

*The rapid growth of our economy in the past two decades has been due mainly to our seizing the opportunities provided by the opening up of the Mainland.* (2003*PA*)

In this example, we can see that besides setting up a positive HK image with rapid growth of economy, the CE here, with the use of temporal prepositional phrase and the perfect tense, tries to attribute the success of HK's economy to Mainland and thus at the same time setting up a positive image of China.

*Hong Kong has finally broken free from the psychological constraints brought about by the colonial era. We should have the courage to set aside past modes of thought and plan Hong Kong's long term future with new vision.* (1997*PA*)

With the use of perfect tense and the phrase of "the colonial era" the CE tries to set up a positive present HK by devaluing the past colonial history. Words and phrases are used to devalue the colonial past like "broke free" "psychological constraint" and "past modes of thought" . Furthermore, the word "colonial" carries with it the negative connotative implication of bloodiness and cruelty. In contrast, the CE set up a present HK with the words like "free", "courage" and "new" which suggest a new start and a new identification of the HK people with China.

To sum up, the strategy with past temporal reference is used to set up a positive image of HK in both the two sub-corpora with the difference consisting in that in the pre-transitional sub-corpus, this strategy is also used to establish a negative China while in the post-transitional sub-corpus it is used to construct a positive China and at the same time downplay colonial administration in HK.

#### 5. 2. 2. 2 Temporal references indicating the future

Temporal references indicating the future, used to construct a common future, seem to differ to a vast degree in these two sub-corpora. The British Colonial Government tends to use more references indicating the near future without a lot of planning for the far future after 1997.

*Plans are in hand to deal with this problem. The number of hospital beds will increase by no less than* 50% *in the coming decade.* (1987*PA*)

The temporal references in this sentence are the future tense and a prepositional phrase of "the coming decade" . The future that the Governor takes into account is only a decade from the year 1987, which indicates that the Government would not consider the future beyond that moment. Thus future in this sentence is restrained with a limit.

*We will do everything that is honorable and sensible to cooperate with China for the remaining thousand days of British rule.* (1994*PA*)

In this sentence, the future tense and the adverb of time indicate not only the limitedness of its sovereignty but also the urgency to accomplish the work before this time limit and uncertainty of this accomplishment. From these two examples of temporal reference as a strategy in the pre-transitional sub-corpus, we can infer that the short-term future of HK is constructed because the British would withdraw its rule from HK in 1997. Thus, in this construction, sense of urgency and uncertainty cannot be avoided.

However, the same type of strategy, temporal references with reference to the future, seems to construct a common new near or far future in the post-transitional sub-corpus.

*In the coming years, we will continue to consolidate the reforms we have already put in place and focus our attention on education and the changes we need to make to health care.* (2000*PA*).

In the above example, we can see the future lying ahead does not have a time limit with the use of the phrase "the coming years", which is quite contrary to that in the pre-transitional sub-corpus.

*Provided we persevere in our endeavours, we firmly believe that we and our next generation will create a more vibrant and prosperous Hong Kong. We will make a success of "One Country, Two Systems" and accomplish the mission that history has entrusted to us in the course of the revival of our great nation* (2004*PA*).

In this example, future tense is employed. The government tries to ensure its people that a bright future is extending without limit, which is the outcome of "One Country, Two System" and also which is attributed to the handover of the sovereignty to China. As a result HK people should contribute to the revival of China. In this way, the future of HK and that of China are incorporated, thus identity incorporated and without time limit.

In sum, the same strategy of future temporal reference is employed in the two sub-corpora with different usages. As is discussed before, be he the Governor or the CE, the addresser of the PA is by definition the custodians of the future of Hong Kong and he should make references to common worries and problem, common aims and plans in order to stimulate the forms of identification, solidarity and union among their people, which is the reason of the use of future temporal references. But the difference of the two sub-corpora lies in that in the pre-transitional PA, a sense of urgency in time and uncertainty and discontinuity of the future can be detected, while in the post-transitional PA, the HKSAR Government tries to ensure its people of the continuation of future and the continuation of their identity incorporated into China.

### 5.2.2.3 Temporal reference of "1997"

The year 1997 is significant in that it marks the sovereignty of HK handed over from the Great Britain to PRC which turned HK from a colony of Britain to a SAR of the PRC. Altogether in our present corpus we've found 247 times of "1997" with the help of antconc 2 with 211 "1997" s in the pre-transitional sub-corpus and another 36 in the post-transitional sub-corpus. Thus, we can see that "1997" plays an important role that it marks the ending of the British Colonial rule and the start of "One Country, Two Systems".

Examples of "1997" in the pre-transitional sub-corpus:

(1) *And we must develop and consolidate our governmental institutions so that they can tackle effectively our immediate problems, be ready for the changes which will take place in* 1997. (1988*PA*)

(2) *On* 1 *July* 1997, *Hong Kong will become a Special Administrative Region of the People's Republic of China.* (1989*PA*)

(3) *But images are often created by events beyond our control. When the name of Hong Kong is mentioned nowadays, far too many people probably think either of* 1997 *or of Vietnamese boat people. We must do what we can to project a more balanced and more positive image of this exciting city.* (1989*PA*)

(4) *Nevertheless, I recognise that civil servants are worried about the future payment of their pensions after* 1997. (1993*PA*)

(5) *The Chinese Government has stated that that Legislative Council cannot continue beyond* 30 *June* 1997 *and that there will have to be new elections... But we have made clear that we do not think there is any good reason to do so..* (1994*PA*)

(6) (... 1997) *... But while I shall be leaving, Britain will not—except in the important constitutional sense—be departing. Britain's moral and political commitment to Hong Kong will remain...* (1996*PA*)

Examples (1) and (2) both link "1997" with "changes" which require effective solution of problems and full preparations; with example (3) the Governor implies that 1997, equal to the HK image, is less positive; in example (4) "1997" suggests worry and uncertainty towards the future; it is suggested in example (5) that the changes in the political system in 1997 is totally unnecessary; while the last example emphasizes the commitment and contribution that Britain has given HK.

Examples of "1997" in the post-transitional sub-corpus:

(7) *On* 1 *July* 1997, *Hong Kong was reunited with China.* (1997*PA*)

(8) *The percentage of primary students enjoying whole-day schooling has risen from* 19% *in* 1997 *to* 32% *this year.* (1999*PA*)

(9) *The major cause of our fiscal deficit lay in the rise in public expenditure during the period of the bubble economy. In the six years between* 1991—1992 *and* 1996—1997, *public expenditure grew on average by* 14% *annually.* (2003*PA*)

(10) *That said, our financial infrastructure is more robust than it was in* 1997. (2008*PA*)

Example (7) shows that HK had been China's and "1997" signifies only a return to its motherland; the contrast in examples (8) and (10) shows the superiority of HK's sovereignty by China to the British rule which is to favor the former by demeaning the latter; while example (9) tries to attribute HK's disadvantage, the fiscal deficit, to the period of time of colonial era.

Based on the above two groups of examples, we can conclude that "1997" is always collocated with negative connotations of the change to be brought about by the transition and used to evoke negative feelings of worry towards the future beyond 1997. Besides this, it is sometimes used to show what Britain has contributed to HK in the 150 years of its colonization of HK. The same temporal reference of "1997" varies its use post-transition. 1997 is the turnover of a historical page in HK's history and an ending of a previous Government which is contrasted in the post-transitional PA to show the superiority of the new page of HK's history after the transition. In other words, "1997" helps construct the advantage of the HKSAR under the Chinese rule and the disadvantage of the colonial era. In conclusion, we can see that this same reference contributes to both a Chinese image and a British image in the two sub-corpora in contrary ways.

This strategy of temporal references is employed in both the sub-corpora to construct the commonness of HK past and future, with the pre-transitional PA focuses more on HK's common past and the post-transitional PA more on HK's common near or distant future. Of the temporal references, "1997" is most significant that it is applied to construct a totally different Britain and China in the two sub-corpora.

### 5.2.3 Spatial reference

In this section, we are to study some lexicons in our corpora that are used to refer to China, Britain and HK which might signify the relations between HK and China, HK and Britain. Strictly speaking, words with references to HK, China and Britain do not belong to spatial references, but this kind of geographical references do indicate the relations. And the three sides in these complicated relations may not only refer to their geographical position, spatial position is the most significant in defining their relationships and the political interests behind them and the powers represented by them. Moreover, according to Wodak (2001), referential strategy is interchangeable with nomination strategy, thus, to examine how the three sides are nominated in our present corpus may embody the relations among them. As discussed above, words with positive connotations will be used to describe the in-group and its qualities whereas words with negative connotations will be used to evoke the out-group and its supposed shortcomings and faults. These antonymous lexical sets are often made up of "value vocabulary" (Chilton, 2004), words that help to establish a dichotomy between a positive in-group versus a negative out-group. Words that are used to refer to China, HK and Britain may give a suggestion of their relations.

**Lexicons with reference to China**

The following table shows the references to China in the pre-transitional and post-transitional sub-corpora respectively and also the times of presence of each reference in the two sub-corpora.

**Table 9 References of "China" in the 22 Policy Addresses**

| Pre-transition | | Post-transition | |
|---|---|---|---|
| References | Times of presence | References | Times of presence |
| China | 302 | the Mainland | 306 |
| the Chinese Government | 56 | China | 115 |
| Peking | 32 | our country | 60 |
| the Mainland | 11 | the Central Government | 36 |
| the Chinese side | 10 | our motherland | 19 |
| the People's Republic of China | 8 | the Central Authorities | 8 |
| the Central Government | 1 | Beijing | 8 |
| | | the central people's government | 6 |
| | | our nation | 3 |
| | | People's Republic of China | 1 |

In the pre-transitional corpus, the first six lexicons denoting China are neutral which may be allowed to be used in the same way to refer to any other country like the U. S., the US Government, Washington, etc. with an exception of the last one because to a Governor who is British it is an awkward way to refer to another opposing government the Central Government. The original sentence goes like this: Another area which has been the subject of much debate is the relationship between the Central Government and the SAR Government (1989PA, p. 43). It is evident that this reference is used to show the future relationship of HK and China, and thus spoken in the voice of the future HK government.

In the post-transitional sub-corpus, we have some lexicons referring to China common to the pre-transitional sub-corpus which are considered to be neutral: the Mainland, China, Beijing and the People's Republic of China. A little less neutral are lexicons of the Central Authorities and the Central People's Government, which indicate that HK is subordinated to China and thus China is "central" with HK positioned as "local". Lexicons that are more positively connotative are "our country" and "our nation" which show total integration of HK into China and HK as a part of the country. The most highly connotative is the reference "our motherland" which compares China to one's mother and thus the most emotional in the sense that China is the ancestral country (Zuguo in Chinese). Most interestingly, the spelling of "Beijing" conforms to the Chinese PinYin which also witnesses the HKSAR Government's identification with the particular usage in China instead of "Peking" used pre-transition.

Therefore, it is clear that the pre-transitional PA uses neutral lexicons to refer to China and takes it as any other country in the world, while the post-transitional PA tends to use highly emotional lexicons with reference to China with positive connotations.

**Lexicons with reference to Britain**

In the pre-transitional sub-corpus, we have:

*the United Kingdom* (6 *times*);
*Her Majesty's Government* (5 *times*);
*the British Government* (3 *times*).

The reference of the British Government may rank quite neutral. When the context of their use is taken into account, they may seem not too neutral. Take 1990PA for example, "the HK Government, the British Government, have tried over the past year..." It can be inferred here that the HK Government is a representative of the British Government, or at least the British Government should be in support of the HK Government, and therefore, the Governor considers HK a part of Britain. Thus, carefully studied, neutral reference may not always be neutral. "the United Kingdom" is less neutral than "the British Government". Further, people non-British would not refer to the British Government with "Her Majesty's Government" which is used to show great respect and total subordination to the British Government. To conclude, the two connotative terms are used more than the neutral term of "the British Government".

In the post-transitional sub-corpus, we hardly have any definite words directly referring to the British Government but from some other phrases referring to the colonial period we still can have a glimpse of how Britain is negatively referred to in the post-transitional PA. The word "colonial" appears 6 times in this sub-corpus in "colonial rule" (two times), "colonial page" (one time), "colonial administration" (one time) and "colonial era" (two times), from which we can infer that Britain becomes colonizer in this sub-corpus. With "colonizer", feelings of dislike or hatred, or connotation of bloodiness of the colonizer, may be evoked and is thus transferred in this reference.

In contrast with the highly emotional and respectful "Her Majesty's Government" in the pre-transitional sub-corpus, the post-transitional PA establish a negative connotation in Britain through the repeated use of "colonial".

**Lexicons with reference to Hong Kong**

In the pre-transitional sub-corpus, we have: Hong Kong; this/our community; the city.

In the post-transitional sub-corpus, we have: Hong Kong; this/our community, the city, the region.

From this references list, it seems that the two sub-corpora use the same category of references to refer to HK if these references are examined independently. However, if context is taken into account, the outcome may not be as simple that the two sub-corpora use the same category of reference for HK, as Beard (2000) notices "groups of words that are related in meaning as a result of being connected with a particular context of use". This comparative study will approach the analysis of the lexical pattern and seek to determine in how far these word choices help construct the identity of HK and its relations to China. Because "Hong Kong" and "this/our community" are intensely neutral and hardly take with them any adjectives, our focus will stay with the other several references.

Firstly, "the region" is only used in the post-transitional sub-corpus to refer to HK, which differs from its usage in the pre-transitional sub-corpus. On the one hand, it may be due to the fact that HK becomes a special administrative region of China after the transition, as a result the HKSAR Government are inclined to refer to HK the region as a short form of the HKSAR. On the other hand, the HKSAR Government's determination of integrating into the development of the PRD (Pearl River Delta) region leads to its frequent use of "the region" as a self-reference, e. g., "we need to broaden our horizons and intensify economic integration with the PRD Region" (2008PA) and also when addressing the importance of HK's integration into the PRD, the CE continues, "HK must pull its strengths with other cities in the region" (2003PA). Consequently, the excessive use of "the region" as a self-reference in the post-transitional PA may be attributed to HK's integration into the PRD and the change in HK's denomination into a special region of China. While in the pre-transitional sub-corpus, "the region", is either used to refer to the future HK Government—the HK Special Administration which is to signify the change in the transition and also create uncertainty towards the unknown future or used to show HK's position in the "Asia-Pacific region" as in 1989PA, "the Asia-Pacific region contains the fastest growing economies in the world. Ours is one of them". Thereby, "the region" is not a self-reference but may be equal "the area".

Secondly, the use of "the city" to refer to HK seems identical in the two sub-corpora, but context is also a must in the analysis. In the pre-transitional sub-corpus, "the city" is often used in "a modern city" "an exciting city" "a quiet city" "a safe city" "the business city" "an honest city" "a dynamic city" and "an open city". With so many adjectives modifying "the city", we can also infer that all these contribute to the construction of a positive HK image. However the most frequent adjectives before "the city" are "international" "cosmopolitan" and "world", which not only emphasize HK's position in the world, but HK's not belonging to any one country or nation. It is not the same case with the post-transitional sub-corpus. Besides those adjectives mentioned above, in the post-transitional PA, we further have "a major city in China" "an important city in the PRD region" "a Chinese city" "the city staging the 2008 Olympic Equestrian Events" "the major city within our country", all of which highlight the "Chineseness" of HK. It can be concluded that when "the city" is used to refer to HK, it differs in the present two sub-corpora to a degree that the pre-transitional PA emphasizes the worldness of HK while the post-transitional PA puts further emphasis on HK's Chineseness.

As a referential strategy, lexicons referring to the three places—China, Britain and HK vary to a vast degree in the two sub-corpora. The pre-transitional sub-corpus sets up a favorable relationship between HK and Britain, with HK-China's relationship in a sense more international and HK a more uniquely independent and international city. Whereas, the post-transitional sub-corpus tends to incorporate eagerly into China and the PRD, a region in south China, by emphasizing on HK's Chineseness, with a breakoff from the previous HK government and British colonial rule.

### 5.2.4 Reference as a micro discursive strategy

Referential strategies, which construct collective identity or relationship, may be conceptualized by discourse producers through representing social actors along temporal or spatial axes to construct an in-group versus an out-group where particular characteristics or values are selected and foregrounded. In this present study, three sub-strategies of referential strategies are examined, namely, personal reference, temporal references and spatial references, which serve to distinguish between the in-group and the out-group. As illustrated, pre-transitional PA constructs China as out-grouped without including China into the personal sphere of "we", focuses on HK's common achievements and contributes little to the distant future of HK, and positions HK more an international and independent city. Besides constructing HK as an international city, the post-transitional corpus places HK more as a Chinese city and hereby identifies it with China and incorporates into China. In addition, positive connotation is attached to lexicons referring to Britain and HK, or the in-grouped in the pre-transitional PA corpus, and highly emotional words are used as references to China and HK, or the in-grouped after Transition. In conclusion, with the same strategies of references, differences in HK identity and different relations between HK and China are constructed.

## 5.3 Rhetorical devices

In a more recent paper, Wodak (2007) claims that a discourse analysis of intricate socio-political problems should be complemented with an analysis of pragmatics or rhetorical devices in the discourse, which proves even more fruitful in contemporary CDA research. Rhetorical devices like allusion and presupposition may be referred to when we are trying to detect and analyse systematically the hidden and coded meanings which may often be covered and neglected without certain contexts.

Further, the concepts of "text, discourse, context and co-text" have to be clarified and theorized in an interdisciplinary framework combining and integrating CDA and pragmatics or rhetorical devices. Although pragmatics has always seen itself as complementary to semantics, as Paul Chilton has clearly illustrated in his book *Analysing Political Discourse* (2004), and research in pragmatics has attempted to distinguish important features of the immediate context (speakers, hearers, settings, expectation, intentions, etc.), these and other relevant dimensions have frequently been left vague or sometimes simply to the researcher's subjective intuition (Reisigl, 2004). On the other hand, much research On CDA has often neglected the subtle and intricate analysis of latent meanings and has left the interpretation of implicit, presupposed and inferred meanings to the intuition of the research and/or the readership, although one of CDA's goals is to uncover the covert relationship or power in discourse. Hereafter, the present research intends to make explicit the implicit through an analysis of the use of rhetorical devices in the PA.

Moreover, an integrative pragmatic and discourse-analytic approach has to be further complemented with a range of other linguistic theoretical concepts as well as with theories from neighbouring disciplines. Such a theoretical framework should not only exist as an "abstract umbrella or general framework", unrelated to the explicit and concrete analysis; such a framework would rather be necessary to be able to choose and justify the relevant categories for the analysis itself (van Dijk, 2003; Wodak, 2000)

### 5.3.1 Allusion

According to the Oxford English Dictionary, the term "allusion" may sometimes be used loosely to mean "a covert, implied or indirect reference" (OED). This meaning typically involves hinting at something, often by the use of vague language, rather than mentioning it directly (Ben-Porat, 1976). This sense is found in Dr. Johnson's dictionary (1755), where "allusion" is defined as "that which is spoken with reference to something supposed to be already known, and therefore not expressed; a hint; an implication". But Paul Lennon (2004) defines allusion in a narrower sense as a cover term for a group of language-use phenomena linked more or less strongly to one another by formal, structural characteristics and pragmatic, functional characteristics within the communicative dialogue established between the speaker/writer and hearer/reader. While according to Wikipedia①, allusion is "a figure of speech which makes a reference to, or representation of a place, event, literary work, myth, or work of art, either directly or by implication". Thus the term "allusion" varies from scholar to scholar and is seldom made clear, but standard definitions of it share the idea of "reference to something". The following are some shared characteristics concluded

---

① Wikipedia is a website of encyclopedia. http://en.wikipedia.org/wiki/Portal: Contents

from other literature:

*Assumption of shared background knowledge* (*Kellett*, 1969; *Cicourel*, 1969; *Halliday*, 1978; *Miner*, 1993);

*Implicature on the speaker/writer's part to convey implicit intertextual meaning* (*Coombs*, 1984; *Leppihalme*, 1994);

*Indirectness* (*Brenneis*, 1986);

*Associative reference as opposed to the representational meaning of the surface-text* (*Ben-Porat*, 1976; *Perri*, 1978; *Nadel*, 1982);

*Foregrounding of the elements in the text which bears associative meaning. This may be achieved by various means, particularly by means of lexical substitution* (*Mukarovsky*, 1964; *Lemke*, 1985; *Wilss*, 1989);

*It can become lexicalized and can become fossilized* (*Wilss*, 1989; *Leppihalme*, 1994)

Some studies like Lennon's (2004) consider intertextuality a type of allusion, but the present research distinguishes allusion from intertextuality in that allusion is an intentional effort on the writer's part and the success of an allusion depends in part on its reader's getting it (and intertextuality will be defined in the next section).

Although allusions resemble other types of implicit components of meaning, it is necessary to go into further details and differentiate allusions properly. Januschek provides a useful definition for allusions embedded in political discourse:

*... in contrast to slogans, allusions require active thinking and discriminating recipients. Not everyone can understand allusions, and those who do understand them have to do something about it: they have to give meaning to the allusion. The creator of the allusion can thereby renounce responsibility for the meaning that arises: he may distance himself. In other words: allusions can be very short—but they can never be one-sided communicative acts. And, allusions may be understood in a highly explosive way—but always so subtly that they provoke contradiction and cannot be casually filed away in particular drawers. Whereas electoral slogans tend to cause fragmented discourse to break down completely, allusions drive it forward. Under the conditions of fragmentized political communications they are the linguistic means that relies on the fact that citizens, under these same conditions, generally act intelligently and not merely as puppets for the*

*cleverest manipulators.* (*Januschek*, 1994)

Through allusion, Wodak, et al. (1990) claim that one can suggest and address negative associations and connotations without being held responsible for them. Ultimately the associations are only hinted at; the listeners/viewers/readers must make them explicit in the act of reception (Wodak & de Cillia 1998). Allusions depend on shared knowledge [Searle's (1976) background assumptions, Sperber and Wilsons' (1986) mutual manifestness, van Dijk's (2005) common sense knowledge, and so forth]. The person who alludes to something counts on the general preparedness for resonance of the audience, that is, the hearer's tendency to expand literal meanings according to the shared knowledge.

In the field of politics, allusions may bear the intention, and achieve the result, of devaluating political opponents, without accepting responsibility for what is implicitly said: at best an invitation is given to make particular connections. What is not pronounced creates, in the case of allusions, a kind of secrecy of intimacy, and familiarity suggests something like: "we all know what is meant". The world of experience exists, however, in a "repertoire of collective knowledge", which we can analyse through historical, psychological, etc. studies and theories. Allusions frequently rely on ... topoi (world conspiracy) and standardized linguistic patterns which manifest and carry clearly defined meanings (Mitten, 1992; Wodak, 2004a), or which point to collectively well-established stereotypes. In line with the definition of HK identity in the present research, simply put, to align HK with or alienate HK from China, allusion in this political discourse of PA may be used to value the in-group or devaluate the out-group.

(1) *The tragic events in China had a traumatic effect on Hong Kong: an effect made all the more direct by the impact of television. Much has been written and said about those events, both at the time and since. I do not intend to add to it now. The important point for us is that what happened in China created increased concern about the arrangements for Hong Kong's future. A mark of this was the significant increase in applications for emigration and the widespread demands for the right of abode in the United Kingdom.* (1989*PA*)

In this paragraph, the allusion "the tragic events" refers to something that happened in Mainland China in that year immediately after the death of former CCP General Secretary Hu Yaobang and which, according to Flowerdew (1998), "shattered any confidence that had remained after the signing of the JD". Without explicitly mentioning it, this alluding phrase can be well interpreted by HK people at that time. Words like "tragic" "concern" and "emigration" help interpret this allusion.

(2) *We need to restore mutual trust as the necessary cornerstone for the unprecedented political experiment that will begin in* 1997. (1989*PA*)

The reunification of HK with its Motherland is alluded here to a "political experiment". As experiment may turn out to be successful or failing, the Governor does not hold very hopeful prospects for the future of HK and hence the 1997 transition. Thus at least the sense of uncertainty is attached as a label to the Transition.

(3) *During the Prime Minister's talks in Peking, it was agreed that the Group's work should be speeded up and all necessary resources given to it, so that the building blocks for the post-*1997 *system are firmly in place by that year. The Group should now be in a position to function more efficiently and more quickly than has been possible in the recent past. I very much hope that this will enable it to resolve those issues which are still outstanding between the two sides.* (1991*PA*)

In this example two allusions can be detected, "building blocks" and "those issues". The two allusions refer to an unresolved issue in 1991 concerning the Court of Final Appeal (CFA). The Joint Liaison Group reached an agreement to set up the CFA in 1993 so that by the time of the handover it would be well up and running. In spite of what had been stipulated in both documents (JD/BL) about the number of oversea judges for the CFA, it was decided that there would be a maximum of only one overseas judge who could sit on the Court (Flowerdew, 1998).

(4) *During the consultation exercise conducted over the past three months, the community held animated and extensive discussions on the legislative proposal. I consider this kind of dialogue to be proper and normal.* (2003*PA*)

"The legislative proposal" alludes to the proposal of Article 23 stipulated in the BL which the HKSAR Government is to legislate in the year 2003. Press in HK is to be distinguished under the Article 23 between "reporting" "criticizing/disagreeing" and "advocating", the latter being forbidden and defending a policy such as the independence for Taiwan would be seen as constituting "action" and their proponents could therefore be faced with penalties. Thus, such a proposal may seem a constraint by some on the freedom of press in HK and it is as such alluded to with "the legislative proposal" without explicit naming it or explanation of its content.

(5) *To better ensure food safety, the Government has been working on a comprehensive Food Safety Bill for introduction in the current legislative session. The recent milk product incidents have highlighted the inadequacies of existing laws and the need to speed up the legislative work.* (2008*PA*)

"Milk product incidents" alludes to the events originating in China that a substance, melamine which is a cheap additive that looks like protein in tests, is supplemented to animal feed and milk, even though it does not provide any nutritional benefits. This event is considered to be one of China's food safety scandals, with reports in HK newspaper stating, "HK people have been eager to embrace ancestors of blood, but their ancestors always make them humiliated". This may interpret the alluded milk product incidents.

All the above five allusions suggest some negative associations or connotations of the China side, but they differ in their use. Example (1) alludes to the events taking place in China without explicitly mentioning it, which shows that the HK government at that time would like to distance itself from holding responsible for their words because in that same year HK was warned by Jiang Zemin, the new CCP General Secretary, not to interfere in Mainland affairs with the proverb: "The well water does not interfere with the river water" (Flowerdew, 1998). Example (2) tries to attach some negative value to the transition which was put forward and demanded by Mainland China and thus the negative value to China and devaluate China as an opponent. Example (3) refers to some issues in contention between HK and China, thus putting China on the opposite side of HK and derogatorily labeling China. The fourth and the fifth allusions can be considered to some degree as understatements. Example (4) tries to minimize the negative connotation of the legislature proposal of Article 23 that brings to HK people and example (5) tries to touch lightly on the events of milk in China. In conclusion, all the examples connote some negative value towards China, while in the first three allusions, either the British Colonial HK Government wants to distance from being held responsible for its words or the Government attempts to attach some negative value to its opponent China. The (4) and (5) allusions implicate something unpleasant concerning China but through minimization such unpleasantness is understated. Thus allusion is considered an effective strategy in the construction or presentation of HK-China relationship with its different uses. It also involves manipulation—in the pre-transitional PA, it is used to attach negative value to China while holding irresponsible for the statements; in the post-transitional PA, it is used to minimize the unpleasantness and reduce the negativeness of China and thus to set up a more positive China image. In this way, allusion can be used with contradictory effects—to attach negativeness to the out-group or to reduce negativeness of the in-group. It can be further inferred that allusion can be a way of manipulation in discourse.

### 5.3.2 Presupposition

Whereas allusion requires some background knowledge, presupposition is a strategy that it demands more on the listeners/readers' language knowledge to identify it. The concept of presupposition is central to linguistics and pragmatics. The German mathematician and logician Gottlob Frege is generally recognized as the first scholar in modern times who introduced the philosophical study of presupposition (Frege, 1892), though the notion of presupposition may go back at least as far as the medieval philosopher Petrus Hispanus (Horn, 1996). Since its introduction, presupposition has attracted an ever-growing amount of attention from both philosophers and linguists. In linguistics, the investigation of presupposition is concerned with a wide range of phenomena, centering around the general debates about the interaction and division of labour between semantics and pragmatics, but Soames (1989) sums up that "theories of presupposition are neither exclusively semantic nor exclusively pragmatic, but rather require the integration of both kinds of information".

Presupposition is defined as "a heterogeneous collection of quite distinct and different phenomena" by Levinson (1983). Huang (2007) defines presupposition in his Pragmatics in this way: presupposition can be informally defined as an inference or proposition whose truth is taken for granted in the utterance of a sentence. Its main function is to act as a precondition of some sort for the appropriate use of that sentence.

The analysis of presuppositions with speech act theory, which began with John

Ausin (1961) and John Searle (1969, 1976), makes it possible to make explicit the implicit assumptions and intertextual relations that underlie text production (Schiffin, 1994). Strawson's (1950) notion of presupposition gives rise to the notion of logical presupposition defined as follows: Sentence S1 semantically presupposes sentence S2 if and only if sentence S1 entails sentence S2 and the negation of sentence S1 also entails S2. If S2 is false, then S1 is neither true nor false. In other words, it has no truth value. There are many linguistic phenomena that are related to presuppositions. Yule (1996), concentrates on the following types.

**Table 10 Types of presupposition**

| Type | Example | Presupposition |
|---|---|---|
| Existential | "the X" | X exists. |
| Factive | "I regret having done that" | I did it. |
| Non-factive | "he claimed to be a teacher" | He was not a teacher. |
| Lexical | "She managed to escape" | She attempted to escape. |
| Structural | "Who is coming?" | Someone is coming. |
| Counter-factual | "if I were not ill..." | I am ill. |

A presupposition of a sentence must normally be part of the common ground of the utterance context (the shared knowledge of the interlocutors) in order for the sentence to be felicitous. Sometimes, however, sentences may carry presuppositions that are not part of the common ground and nevertheless be felicitous. For example, in the sentence, "President Clinton's liberal views are not popular with many Congressional Republicans", it is presupposed that President Clinton has "liberal" views. In this case, it is the possessive form (Clinton's) that triggers the presupposition; many other kinds of linguistic constructions can also serve as presupposition triggers. This process of an addressee assuming that a presupposition is true, even in the absence of explicit information that it is, is usually called presupposition accommodation. We have just seen that presupposition triggers like Clinton's (possessive form) allow for such accommodation. Presupposition is a type of linguistic device that can be used at the word/phrase/sentence level to manipulate readers. These are words or phrases or sentences that assume the truth of the statements in which they are found as shown in the above figure.

It is useful to notice, for further analyses, that presuppositions have remarkable properties regarding the triggering of audience consent to the message expressed. Presupposed content is, under ordinary circumstances, and unless there is a cautious interpretive attitude on the part of the hearer, accepted without much critical attention. Presupposition, according to Wodak (2007), is a very effective way to manufacture consent and thus a highly manipulative persuasive strategy. Therefore presupposition, according to Wodak, et al. (2008), is useful in deconstructing a text but requires a close analysis of the context and most suitable in a critical study of discourse.

In the data of our present research, presupposition is used to pave the way of instilling a positive or negative image of China and thus qualifying or disqualifying the Chinese government or Chinese values. Too many presuppositions are in our data, because without presupposition, communication would be impossible. What we are going to analyse is those suppositions that contribute to the construction of HK identity—to align HK with China or to alienate HK from China.

Presupposition in the pre-transitional PA sub-corpus:

(1) *For many years our community has recognised the importance of not becoming directly involved in China's often complicated domestic politics.* (1989*PA*)

In this sentence, we have the following presupposions: not becoming directly involved in China's often complicated domestic politics is important; China's domestic politics is often complicated. The original sentence presupposes a negative image of China and Chinese government, which is also turned into the reason of asking the HK people to detach from China. If a reader can not identify these two presuppositions here, he may only realize that he should not keep close ties with China which he is persuaded to do without telling him that this is a persuasion as well as a warning.

(2) *In our evolving relationship with China, there are still, inevitably, stresses and strains which can only be overcome by mutual effort and mutual understanding.* (1990*PA*)

(3) *The Memorandum of Understanding shows that with patience, perseverance and goodwill, even the most difficult problems in our relationship with China can be overcome.* (1991*PA*)

The above two examples both presuppose the relationship between HK and China is difficult because there exist stresses and strains. Thus in this way, China is placed in the opposite side to HK, or as an opponent which negative connotations may be suggested, or in other words, our HK opponent, here China, is attached with a label of the qualities of what we don't like or lack of the qualities of what we prefer.

(4) *There is precious little to be said for wasting time and breath on public recrimination about who is most to blame for the snail's pace of Joint Liaison Group work.* (1994*PA*)

It presupposes that the JLG's work has been too slow, whose responsibility surely lies in the China's side as the Governor addresses in an earlier paragraph, "the volume of the work which remains to be done in the JLG ... is formidable. We will continue to impress on our Chinese colleagues the urgency of the task and our willingness to co-operate fully with China to accomplish that task" which is to exempt HK from being criticized for the slow work of the JLG and makes China to shoulder all responsibility and thus China becomes the hindrance in the progress of the JLG's work.

(5) *We will, however be as unequivocal in a positive direction in the help that we give to the Chief Executive (Designate).* (1996*PA*)

"*It is sometimes suggested that we would give more help to a successful candidate whom we had favoured over other rivals for this onerous post. That is nonsense. We have no candidate. The selection is not for us. We have not, will not, and would not seek to interfere in the selection process*". (1996*PA*)

Such sentences in the last PA of the last Governor presuppose that the election of the first CE is the selection of China or designated by China, and it is not a selection of HK because among the sixty members of the Provisional Legislature, fifty-one were members of the Selection Committee; thirty-three of them were members of pro-Beijing political groups which reduced the credibility of this body for the HK public. The selection process got heavily criticized by Chris Patten the last Governor by calling it "a bizarre farce" (Hong Kong Standard, Dec. 22th, 1996). Thus by presupposing that the election of the first CE is a selection of China, the PA tries to attach a negative label to China of lacking of democracy and of no right in election.

Based on the above five expositions of presupposition in the pre-transitional sub-corpus, the conclusion can be drawn that anything connected with China can be negatively presupposed: China's politics is too complex to get involved; China is an opponent of HK which imposes strain and stresses on the HK-China relations; China is an obstacle in the preparatory work of the transition; China is without democracy.

Presupposition in the post-transitional sub-corpus:

In the post-transitional PA sub-corpus, the most evident and prominent presupposition is the existential type: the X presupposes the existence of X. A lot of expositions could be found like "the success of China" "the fast development of Mainland" "the achievements of our motherland" which contribute to the construction of a successful China with fast developments and vast achievements. Some other lexical presuppositions like "the reunification with our motherland" could be detected in many places of this sub-corpus presupposing that HK was once China's and the handover of sovereignty was nothing but a natural return of HK to its motherland.

(1) *Hong Kong's reunification with China under the "One Country, Two Systems" concept requires us to appreciate and accept one practical and profound truth: Hong Kong's prosperity and stability are closely linked with those of the Mainland.* (1997*PA*)

This statement presupposes "one practical and profound truth", that is, HK's prosperity and stability are closely linked with those of the Mainland, which is not only to in-group China, but attaches a label of positive quality of China with which HK owes its "prosperity and stability" to China and which is also the linkage between the two sides.

(2) *Overcoming the challenges faced in the past two years has not been easy. It has only been possible because of the perseverance, initiative and pragmatism shown by Hong Kong people and the ample trust and full support shown by our country.* (1999*PA*)

This statement presupposes that "our country has shown ample trust and full support to us" which further presupposes that "we belong to one country". The presupposition as a rhetorical strategy here helps integrate HK into China and also indicate the drive to overcoming the Asian turmoil is from China—the ample trust and full support, which in turn sets up a positive image of China through its help granted to HK.

(3) *This will enable us to make more timely and effective contributions to the development of our country while maintaining Hong Kong's irreplaceable role in the course of national development.* (2007*PA*)

It is presupposed that "we are making timely and effective contributions to the development of our country" which is to reconfirm the words previously addressed "China prospers, and Hong Kong prospers". It is also in line with the previous exposition of presupposition in that HK should make contributions to China because of "what China has granted us".

(4) *The timetable for universal suffrage set by the NPCSC last year enjoys wide support in the community.* (2008*PA*)

(5) *Building a democratic system on a shared sense of national identity is where our future lies.* (2008*PA*)

Expositions (4) and (5) both presuppose some political truth. Exposition (4) presupposes that "we have a timetable of universal suffrage" and (5) "we have a democratic system which is based on a shared sense of national identity". As is known, democracy and freedom are what HK people cherish and are proud of, which are offered by "our country" and "our shared national identity" of being Chinese. In this way, China is credited for HK's democracy and freedom.

From the above five expositions of presupposition in the post-transitional sub-corpus, it can be inferred that a positive image of China is built with its prosperity, its trust, support and what it has offered to HK's democracy.

In conclusion, presupposition is also highly manipulative in that what the governments want to instill its people with is presupposed to be truth and shared knowledge, which is subconsciously accepted.

### 5.3.3 Rhetoric as a micro discursive strategy

As is analysed above, the two rhetorical devices of allusion and presupposition are powerful strategies in the discursive construction of HK identities in the two sub-corpora of PA. The textual and pragmatic analysis, embedded in the contextual analysis of discourses and discourse strands demonstrates that such strategies can be cognitively and emotionally effective if the contents of the various levels of contextual and cotextual assumptions are involved. In this particular case, it demonstrates the extent to which the PA has used allusion and presupposition in the construction of either a positive image or a negative image of China. What is also relevant to our discussion is the evidence that the CDA approach to the particular discourse of PA needs a variety of neighboring disciplines of some background knowledge of society, economy and politics. Rhetorical devices, considered traditionally to be aiming at the explanation of micro phenomena at the level of sequential interpretation of utterances, can take discourse into account as complex and contextualized speech events and thus become discursive strategies in discourse studies. Both of the two rhetorical strategies analysed in the present section are highly manipulative and thus a form of persuasion (Dillard & Pfau, 2002; O'Keefe, 2002; Wang & Shen, 2016).

## 5.4 Intertextuality

The notion of intertextuality offers a perspective of both reading and writing texts as a way of looking at a text's interactions with prior texts, writers, readers, and conventions. It embodies the idea that no utterance is in any real sense new, but that every utterance is a response to and built on past utterances. As a result, every text is intertextual (Fairclough, 1992).

### 5.4.1 Intertextuality in the present study

Fairclough suggests that analysing discourse types may involve complex configurations of several genres and several discourses. Discourse, in Fairclough's words (1995b), is "a particular way of constructing a particular (domain of) social practice", and genre is "a way of using language which corresponds to the nature of the social practice that is being engaged in". By analysing intertextuality, researchers aim to specify which fields (topics, subject-matters) are associated with a genre, and which discourses are drawn upon to construct these fields. Fairclough defines intertextuality basically as "the property texts have of being full of snatches of other texts, which may be explicitly demarcated or merged in, and which the text may assimilate, contradict, ironically echo, and so forth" (Fairclough, 1992a).

In this study, Bazerman's (2004) perspective on intertextuality is employed as the point of departure to analyse the intertextual practices. Bazerman's (2004) distinguishes different levels at which a text invokes another text and relies on the other text as a resource. He identifies six levels of intertextuality that emerge in a text. These are "prior text as a source of meaning to be used at face value" "explicit social dramas of prior texts engaged in discussion" "background, support, and contrast" "beliefs, issues, ideas, statements generally circulated" "recognizable kinds of language, phrasing and genre", and "resources of language". These levels of intertextuality can be recognized through certain techniques that represent the words and utterances of others. These techniques start with the most explicit —"direct quotation" and "indirect quotation"; to "mentioning of a person, document, or statements" and "comment or evaluation on a statement, text, or otherwise invoked voice"; to more implicit "using recognizable phrasing, terminology associated with specific people or groups of people or particular document" and "using language and forms that seem to echo certain ways of communicating, discussions among other people, types of documents". What we refer to by using the term intertextuality is the manifest intertextuality in the form of quotation with overt surface signals of quotation marks because implicit intertextuality may be controversial in that it may lead to subjectivity. Hence, in this study, quotation and intertextuality are used interchangeably.

### 5.4.2 Intertextuality, voice and identity construction

Intertextuality relates to the sourcing of propositions or claims. While introducing the voice of others, the writer of a text "is simultaneously required to take up a speaking/writing position, to comment on, evaluate, and position themselves in relation to those words" (Baynham, 1999), so as to justify mentioning the other. That is, the writer has to choose what to cite and what position to take to the introduced voice. In this sense, two groups of voices are involved in intertextuality: the writer voice and the quoted voice. As Bakhtin (1978) puts it:

*... an author may utilize the speech act of another in pursuit of his own aims and in such a way as to impose a new intention on the utterance, which nevertheless retains its own proper referential intention. Under these circumstances and in keeping with the author's purpose, such an utterance may be recognized as originating from another addresser. Thus, within a single utterance, there may occur two intentions, two voices.* (*Bakhtin*, 1978)

Bakhtin's argument implies that the voices involved in intertextuality are not independent. In fact, they are hierarchical in the sense that it is the writer that makes the decision as to whose voice is being allowed to intrude into his/her texts and how to organize these voices to achieve certain communicative purposes. As is further stated by Bazerman (2004), "intertextuality is not just a matter of which other texts you refer to, but how you use them, what you use them for, and ultimately how you position yourself as a writer to them to make your own statement". Intertextuality, then, offers a bridge or interface between the context and the text. In the case of the present study, intertextuality is crucial to understanding what other resources are involved in the governments' Policy Addresses which may explicitly signals the governments' attitude—to align HK with or to alienate HK from the sourc voice. Through the intertextual process of adopting the discourse of the community the HK governments may identifying with the discourse community. Thus intertextuality is a most important strategy in the construction of identity.

In this study we are to follow the procedures proposed by Bazerman (2004) for analyzing intertextuality:

(1) Create a list of all instances of intertextuality in the text, that is, to evaluate the material as relevant;

(2) List how the instance is expressed, that is, to evaluate the degree of textual integration (i. e., whether it is through a direct quotation, indirect quotation, paraphrase or description);

(3) Identify whether it is attributed to some person or source;

(4) Interpret the intertextuality, that is, make comments on how or for what purpose the intertextual element is being used in the text.

In the above procedures, step (2) is to be omitted because what is taken into consideration is only direct quotation. In our following analysis, we will list all the instances of intertextuality in our two sub-corpora and categorize them according to their sources or uses.

### 5.4.3 Intertextuality in the PAs before transition

After careful study of the intertextual expositions in this pre-transition corpus, according to the different sources, intertextuality in this corpus can be categorized into three groups: 1) quotations of proper names in accepted usage of both the speaker and the listeners; 2) quotations of people outside HK, but not Chinese; 3) quotations of the Basic Law (henceforth, BL). We are going into details of these three groups with all the intertextual expositions listed and categorized.

Proper names/familiar language use are following:

(1) *Last year a Committee was appointed, under the Chairmanship of Sir Sze-yuen Chung, to plan our third university : "The Hong Kong University of Science and Technology".* (1987*PA*)

(2) *These are the "sandwich class" families who face special difficulty.* (1992*PA*)

(3) *I intend that members of the public should be involved in overseeing performance pledges through "Users' Committees" where these would help to ensure effective monitoring.* (1992*PA*)

(4) *... These policies can be summed up in a simple rule... the "living within your means" principle of public expenditure....* (1995*PA*)

(5) *We must find a new strategy, one that applies the "user-pays" principle to our road system.* (1995*PA*)

(6) *... The surest way to destroy the market value of a "Made in Hong Kong" label.* (1995*PA*)

In the above six examples, (1) to (5) are proper names in accepted usage by HK people, in which way, the commonness of the people in this community is constructed in that they share some expressions that particularly belong to them. While example (6) not only constructs commonness, but also attaches some degree of value to this intertextual phrase. Actually, "Made in Hong Kong" is a phrase that is neutral in meaning, but when it appears in concordance with "market value" it is rendered some valuable quality and a positive HK image is as such built. Thus the purpose of this category of intertextuality is to construct commonness and a positive HK image.

Quotations of people outside HK are following:

(1) *A rash of recent incidents involving potentially dangerous incursions by Chinese vessels into Hong Kong's territorial waters highlights the importance of cross-border co-operation. If China is worried about smuggling, I can say without equivocation—"so are we". But the right way to deal with this problem is through planned, sensitive and effective co-operation between properly controlled forces, acting within their own boundaries.* (1992*PA*)

(2) *We have taken the pragmatic option of doing what we can to build the airport,*

*as I said last year, "not for Britain, but for Hong Kong and Southern China" . But this pragmatism will not build the whole Airport Core Programme. The date is not far off when the start of some key airport contracts will be held up if we cannot secure the Chinese Government's agreement on financing.* (1993*PA*)

(3) *My favourite political philosopher is Alexis de Tocqueville and of all his wise perceptions about the world this one (which I have quoted before) conveys the essence of Hong Kong's story: "Do you want to test whether a people is given to industry and commerce?", he asked. "Do not sound its ports, or examine the wood from its forests or the produce of its soil. The spirit of trade will get all these things and, without it, they are useless. Examine whether this people's laws give men the courage to seek prosperity, freedom to follow it up, the sense and habits to find it, and the assurance of reaping the benefit".* (1996*PA*)

(4) *Let me quote a few statements from the International Monetary Fund's recent report on Hong Kong:*

*"... no adjustments to the basic policy framework are required at this stage. Indeed, the main challenge will be to resist pressures to adopt a more interventionist approach to policy making."*

*"... In the event, policy actions over the past year have given little reason to doubt the authorities' commitment to their underlying approach."*

*"... [Our] staff agrees with the basic non-interventionist thrust of fiscal policy."*

*"... On the unemployment front, the authorities have resisted calls for activist macroeconomic measures, focusing instead on the microeconomic aspects of the problem. The staff views this approach as appropriate."*

*"... the staff has been encouraged by the widely-held confidence and optimism concerning Hong Kong's prospects—both of which are well justified given the authorities' ongoing commitment to sound policies."*

*Most of the world's Finance Ministers would give their limousines for an endorsement like that.* (1996*PA*)

(5) *These are not British rights. Or European. Or Western. These are not alien concepts irrelevant for Asia and Asians. They are universal, valued as much by men and women in Asia as by their counterparts elsewhere on the planet. Listen to Aung San Suu Kyi, Burma's Nobel Laureate: "It is a puzzlement... how concepts which recognise the inherent dignity and the equal and inalienable rights of human beings, which accept that all men are endowed with reason and conscience and which recommend a universal spirit*

*of brotherhood, can be inimical to indigenous values*". (1996*PA*)

(6) *I have spent my entire career engaged in a political system based on representative democracy. It would be surprising if that had not marked me. It has. I have always been moved by Isaiah Berlin's description of democracy as "the view that the promotion of social justice and individual liberty does not necessarily mean the end of all efficient government; that power and order are not identical with a straitjacket of doctrine, whether economic or political; that it is possible to reconcile individual liberty—a loose texture of society—with the indispensable minimum of organising and authority*". (1992*PA*)

Example (1) and (2) are the voice of the Governor personally, which can also be considered to be the HK government's voice in responding to China's queries on smuggling and the construction of the HK airport. Example (1) is to call for co-operation from the Chinese side. Example (2) is an answer to Chinese protest in the construction claiming that capital in HK is flowing out. The two examples of personal voice are to justify the HK government. Thus in this way, the ingroup-outgroup distinction is demarcated and the justification of the in-group is contrasted with the disjustification of the out-group, with HK the justified in-group and China the disjustified out-group.

In example (3), in order to justify his quotation, the Governor first evaluates the quoted voiced by "my favorite" and "wise perceptions", in this way, the intertextual voice is highly supported that HK's spirit of trade leads to its success.

Intertextual expression (4) is to construct a positive HK fame in quoting the international Monetary Fund's high appraisal of HK, which is furthered by "Most of the world's Finance Ministers would give their limousines for an endorsement like that." Thus a positive HK is constructed in the widely recognized image in the intertexuality.

(5) and (6) are intertextual expositions deployed to justify the political reform of the HK government. (5) quotes the Nobel Laureate's comment on the right of election which the Governor regards as a universal right instead of belonging only to the Western world in support of an elected Legco. (6) is intertextualized in the same way as (5) in gaining support for his "entire career" of democracy and liberty. Two purposes are concluded in the two examples: to promote his own concept and to justify his political reform, which in turn connote the common HK positive.

(3) to (6) are quotations of elites or dependable sources to render

authoritativeness to his concept and his policies. Furthermore, the authoritativeness helps construct a positive HK government and the achievements that are considered to belong to the whole community.

In conclusion, intertextuality of this source renders justification for what the Governor and his government have done (Chen & Wang, 2014). This category of intertextuality sources its justification from people outside HK or international elites, which also in another sense, constructs an international and unique identity for the HK people because the stickyard is international. And for the reason that China is out-grouped, China is constructed as unjustified for what it has done.

Quotations of the Basic Law are following:

(1) *We do not yet have full democracy here in Hong Kong. But democracy is the road which the Chinese Government has agreed Hong Kong should follow. The Joint Declaration lays down that "the legislature of the Hong Kong Special Administrative Region shall be constituted by elections". It also prescribes that the executive "shall be accountable to the legislature". There can be no doubt, therefore, that we are destined to be moving firmly in the direction of democracy.* (1993*PA*)

(2) *Our first duty, to quote from the Joint Declaration, has been "maintaining and preserving the economic prosperity and social stability of Hong Kong". This phrase has been quoted so often in the past ten years that it is in danger of becoming a cliché. But back in* 1984, *the maintenance of Hong Kong's prosperity and stability looked to some like a pretty tall order.* (1994*PA*)

(3) *British Ministers have, also drawn Chinese leaders' attention to the provisions of paragraph* 4 *of the Joint Declaration. I quote: "The Government of the United Kingdom and the Government of the People's Republic of China declare that, during the transitional period between the date of the entry into force of the Joint Declaration and* 30 *June* 1997, *the Government of the United Kingdom will be responsible for the administration of Hong Kong with the object of maintaining and preserving its economic prosperity and social stability; and that the Government of the People's Republic of China will give its cooperation in this connection." That statement could not be much plainer.* (1996*PA*)

(4) *One Country, Two Systems.* (1988, 1989, 1991, 1992, 1992, 1993, 1993, 1993, 1995, 1995*PA*)

The first example is quoted from the BL to justify what has been reformed or what will be reformed in the election because the reformation has been oppugned and protested by the Chinese side. (2) and (3) cite nearly the same to show the achievements of HK government and HK people and to refute some prediction or prophesy that "nothing but trouble ahead" (1996PA) after signing the Joint Declaration. Thus this category of intertextuality constructs a positive HK Colonial Government and also the achievements of HK people in the 10 years since the Joint Declaration. The fourth example will be compared to its counterpart in Section 5.4.5.

This category, quotations of the BL, tries to seek support from the BL to justify the policies that the government is implementing which stirred the CPG a lot (Flowerdew, 1998)

### 5.4.4 Intertextuality in PAs post-transition

In this sub-corpus, intertextuality can also be grouped into three categories. The first category is some proper names widely accepted and commonly used in this community, like "Senior Citizen Residence Scheme" (1997PA) "District Council" (1998PA) "bubble economy", and the fuel price "quick going up, slow going down" (2008PA) to show the commonness in the community, and others like the theme "Hong Kong, Our Home" (1997PA) indicating unification within the community, a "Senior Citizen Residence Scheme" (1997PA) a positive image of HK government in carrying out the schemes, "Asia's Best" Dragon's Back Trail (2005PA), and our reputation as a "shopping paradise" and "gourmet paradise" (2004PA) not only to show commonness of HK but emphsise positive commonness of HK with the words like "best" "paradise", etc.

The second category of intertextuality may be used to promote some administrative concept of the HKSAR Government, whose source may be the supposedly commonly accepted truth by the CE or the quotation of the CE's own words. They are as follows:

(1) *I presented my thoughts on the administration of Hong Kong in my platform entitled "Building a 21st Century Hong Kong Together".* (1999*PA*)

—it is used to construct common future of the community.

(2) *We will explore possible new measures under the themes of "helping to start a new business", "helping to build a new business" and "helping to expand a business".* (2000*PA*)

—it is used to construct a positive HK government image.

(3) *The important goal of "Learning for Life—Learning Through Life" is now widely accepted by the community.* (2000*PA*)

"*to implement the principle of "teaching students according to their aptitude" more effectively*". (2000*PA*)

—the administrative concept is intertextualized as common goal of the community of HK.

(4) *Four years ago, when I stood for election as Chief Executive, I presented my vision for Hong Kong entitled "Building a 21st Century Hong Kong Together" . In my manifesto I said, "I see a stable, equitable, compassionate and democratic society with clarity of direction and unity of purpose; I see an increasingly affluent and well-educated population, proud of our new identity and our Chinese heritage; I see an economy that is one of the most important in the world; I see Hong Kong, as a Special Administrative Region of China, making significant contributions as China emerges as a leader amongst the community of nations." This vision was well-received.* (2000*PA*)

—here the quotation shows the kind of supposed truth by the CE—a positive HK image, HK people's satisfaction of their new Chinese identity, HK's contribution to China, and a positive China image.

(5) *Following the principle of "big market, small government", we have to reduce business costs.* (2003*PA*)

—in which the principle is presupposed to be widely accepted in the community, and also in the next example: We will adhere to our "big market, small government" policy. (2003PA)

(6) *Over the past few years I have been saying, "When Hong Kong succeeds, China will benefit. When China succeeds, Hong Kong will prosper".* (2003*PA*)

—it is an example of the construction of the common fate of HK and China which places China in-grouped with HK, and China is thus discursively built to be positive.

(7) *In previous Policy Addresses, I have explained my thoughts on economic development, and established the strategic direction of "leveraging on the Mainland, engaging ourselves globally, capitalising on our advantages, strengthening our core industries, deploying new knowledge and new technologies and moving up the value chain" . We are promoting Hong Kong as Asia's world city, on par with the role that New York plays in North America and London in Europe.* (2004*PA*)

— in the construction of a positive HK, this quotation at the same time establish a positive China by proposing China to be the leverage and thus in-grouped.

(8) *In formulating policies, we fell short of "thinking what people think" and "addressing people's pressing needs".* (2005*PA*)

—it is the supposedly accepted administrative concept in order to depict a positive HK government and its policies.

(9) *On various occasions, I have explained what I mean by "strong governance". At the Question and Answer Session of the Legislative Council last March, I explained that "the concept of 'strong governance' does not mean that the government is omnipotent. Instead, it is our faith in a small, but strong and effective government that can rise up to challenges, operate with transparency and provide effective response at crucial times". The purpose of strong governance is to serve the people.* (2006*PA*)

—it is the supposedly accepted administrative concept in order to depict a positive HK government and its policies.

(10) *In that Policy Address, entitled "A New Direction for Hong Kong", I advocated "Progressive Development" as a core value of our governance.* (2008*PA*)

—it is the supposedly accepted administrative concept in order to depict a positive HK government and its policies.

In the above 10 quotations, it is evident that the government's policies are supposed to bring good to its people and in this way attach a positive label to the government and also its policies and policy-makers. In setting up a positive HK image, the PA tries to place China in an in-grouped circle in that HK and China share the same fate and the same future, as such labels China as positive in-group.

The third category is the type of intertextuality whose source is from the Chinese side. And this category can be further sub-categorized. The first sub-category is the quotation of words that are of conventional Chineseness.

*... declare* 10 *September each year as "Teachers' Day" as a reminder to all of the enduring importance of the teaching profession.* (1997*PA*)

*We will create a national education platform to be known as "Passing on the Torch".* (2008*PA*)

*Environmental protection is an urgent task. But as an old Chinese saying goes, "It takes more than one cold day for the river to freeze three feet deep".* (2000PA)

In the first exposition, 10 September Teachers' Day is a Chinese festival that HK did not celebrate before 1997 and this declaration in 1997PA, right after the transition, demonstrates the eager integration of HK into China in setting the same day for the same purpose. The intertextuality in the second example is also typical of its Chineseness as 2008 is an Olympic year of China and "passing the torch" is a national event in this year. The third example, an intertextualized Chinese proverb, proposes the incorporation of HK into China by mentioning their same origin. As is illustrated by Flowerdew (2004), Chineseness is typical of the first HKSAR CE's speech. Intertextuality in this sub-category shows the identification with China and can easily generate that HK people are Chinese.

The second sub-category is the quotation from the Chinese official channel.

*The HKSAR Government held the Economic Summit on "China's 11th Five-Year Plan and the Development of Hong Kong" in September last year.* (2007*PA*)

*The National 11th Five-Year Plan states clearly that "support will be given to Hong Kong's development on fronts such as financial services, logistics, tourism and information services, and the maintenance of Hong Kong's status as an international centre of financial services, trade and shipping". This recognises our dominant industries and their important function in our country's development. In this regard, amongst all the cities in China, Hong Kong's role is unique and irreplaceable.* (2006*PA*)

*Building on past co-operation, the SAR Government and the relevant Mainland authorities have agreed that the "Hong Kong and Mainland Major Infrastructure Projects Co-ordinating Committee" be re-established to handle a number of cross-boundary infrastructure projects between Hong Kong and Guangdong.* (1997*PA*)

The first two examples quoting the Chinese governmental conferences convey the message that what concerns China concerns HK and the third exposition is an example of co-operation between HK and China. It can be figured out that HK is involved in some Chinese national affairs, and the involvement establishes the in-group identity of HK and thus a positive HK implicates a positive Chinese identity.

The third sub-category is the direct quotation of some Chinese officials. An example is found quoting the words of the Chinese President Hu Jintao as follows:

*At the welcoming banquet the HKSAR Government hosted on* 30 *June this year*,

*President Hu Jintao earnestly advised that "we should put more emphasis on national education for the youth in Hong Kong and promote exchanges between them and the young people of the Mainland so that they will carry forward the Hong Kong people's great tradition of loving the motherland and loving Hong Kong".* (2007*PA*)

This quotation here may be taken as a command for HK's incorporation into Mainland and the presupposition in Hu's words is that HK people take "loving the motherland" as a tradition and also "loving the motherland" in some degree equals "loving HK". The message that is transparent here is the equation of a HK identity to a Chinese identity. The third category of intertextuality in the post-transitional PA indicates that, instead of sourcing justification internationally, the HKSAR Government seeks for authoritativeness from China and thus aligns HK with China's values and authorities (Chen & Wang, 2014).

### 5.4.5 A comparison of the intertextuality of "One Country, Two Systems"

This intertextuality, sourced from the BL, appears in the two sub-corpora of PA in different proportion and with totally different connotations.

In the pre-transition sub-corpus, this quotation appears 10 times while in the post-transition corpus, this figure amounts to 44. However, differences lie lesser in the quantity than in their respective contexts. We will take three examples from each of the two corpora for analysis. Examples one to three are from the pre-transition sub-corpus and examples four to six the post-transition:

(1) *Hong Kong is linked to China but, in another important sense, separates from it. That will continue to be the case in the future, under the concept of "One Country, Two Systems".* (1989*PA*)

(2) *"One Country, Two Systems". That is what I wish to see. I must and will stand up for our system. That is my responsibility, but, in the final analysis, the Government can only defend that system, that way of life with the community's support. And I say this to all of you. If we are not prepared to stand up for Hong Kong's way of life today, what chance of doing so tomorrow?* (1993*PA*)

(3) *This does not mean that after 1997 the Hong Kong way of doing things will have to be brought in line with the systems in Peking: Hong Kong's way of doing things, and our own systems, will continue. That is what "One Country, Two Systems" means.* (1991*PA*)

(4) *Hong Kong's reunification with China under the "One Country, Two Systems" concept requires us to appreciate and accept one practical and profound truth: Hong Kong's prosperity and stability are closely linked with those of the Mainland. Also, Hong Kong and China share the same fundamental interests.* (1997*PA*)

(5) *On lst July* 1997, *Hong Kong was reunited with the motherland. The colonial chapter drew to a close and the Hong Kong SAR was born, ushering in a new era of "One Country, Two Systems" and "Hong Kong people administering Hong Kong" with a high degree of autonomy.* (2001*PA*)

(6) *I am confident because after* 10 *years of implementing "One Country, Two Systems", the advantages are there for all to see. Only through leveraging the strengths of our country can we position ourselves globally to create a better future.* (2007*PA*)

The first three examples emphasize more on the difference of HK and China. (1) shows that in a more important sense, HK is separate from China. Example (2) insists that HK's future lies in its difference from Beijing, and in (3) the Governor stresses the difference even after 1997. These three examples stress separation and differences between HK and China. Though cited from the same source of the BL, the last three examples vary from the previous three to a vast degree. The citation of these words in (4) shows HK's reliance on China and the common interests shared by HK and China. From the emotional coloring words of "reunited" and "motherland" in (5), this citation stresses the transformation in HK identity, since HK was "reunited with the motherland", and at the same time enjoys the freedom of autonomy. And the last example connects this citation with the no-need-to-tell advantages. So it can be concluded that this particular quotation from the BL in the PAs before the transition stresses more on the differences which is considered to guarantee HK's future and a negative out-group China is thus constructed. While in the PAs after the transition, this citation tends to show HK's integration into China which is to guarantee HK's prosperity and stability. Further in connection with this citation, commentary words are employed and thus a positive in-group China is constructed.

Thus, we can conclude that the British Colonial HK Government emphasizes on the second half of "One Country, Two Systems" whereas the HKSAR Government stresses on the first half of this "One Country, Two Systems".

### 5.4.6 Intertextuality as a micro discursive strategy

In this section we can comprehend that the two sub-corpora cite from different sources. Proper names, elites and the BL become the three major sources of intertextuality in the pre-transition sub-corpus, which helps construct the sameness of HK people, a positive HK government, and a positive HK image with great achievements. The intertexuality of some international elites by some international standards indicates that HK is international. The quotations in the post-transition sub-corpus are mainly some proper names that are commonly used in the community of HK, some administrative concepts or policies by the government to justify this government and to build a positive government image, and also some words from the Chinese side to display the commonness in interests of HK with China and to construct China as ingrouped and thus positive. The quotation of the Chinese Government and Chinese leaders shows that the Chineseness of HK is emphasized in this sub-corpus. The specific citation of "One Country, Two Systems" in the two sub-corpora is of particular significance for its being the core concept of the BL. The PA before Transition emphasizes on the "Two Systems" of this concept and highlights the differences between HK and China and alienates HK from China; while the PA after transition focuses on the "One Country", and the sameness and integration into China and thus results in a positive in-grouped China. To conclude, intertextuality can be manipulative in that what to intertextualized, in other words, the sources of intertextuality, can be manipulative. Even when the sources of intertextuality are the same, as in "One Country, Two Systems", the way to intertextualize can result in different functions.

## 5.5 A summary

In this chapter, a detailed analysis is conducted on the three types of micro-strategies in terms of referential strategies, rhetorical strategies and intertextuality. With the three micro-strategies, China, out-grouped in the pre-transitional sub-corpus, is devalued and distanced and HK is positioned as an international centre by international standard. In the post-transitional sub-corpus, China is constructed as in-group and evaluated as HK's mother country from whom HK gains its firm support and reliance. In seeking for authoritativeness and justification of the HKSAR Government's policies the PA resorts to China as its only source. And in this way HK is constructed with its Chineseness. From the analysis, the three micro-strategies are proved penetrative and revealing.

In conclusion, the referential strategies, rhetorical strategies and intertextual strategies are employed in the construction of the HK identities in the two sub-corpora of PA. Through the analysis, it is evident that the construction of positive in-group and negative out-group is the outcome of manipulation, as stated by van Dijk's (2006). Manipulation, according to van Dijk (2006), is a social phenomenon because it involves the addresser and the addressee, a cognitive phenomenon because it implies the manipulation of the minds of the participants, and also a discursive phenomenon because it is exercised through text. And the construction of HK identities in the sub-corpora of PA consists of the three dimensions of society, cognition and discourse.

# Chapter 6　Transition of Sovereignty, Transition of HK Identity

In this chapter, based on the research results and analyses of the previous two chapters, we intend to discuss the discursive construction of HK identities pre-vs. post-transition and further investigate the discursive identity construction with theories in CDA. This chapter commences with a description of the identity construction in pre-transitional PA and post-transitional PA. Based upon the descriptions and analyses, the discursive construction of identity is discussed in detail along three dimensions in CDA, namely, power, ideology and history. Then the chapter concludes with a summary offered in Section 6. 3.

## 6. 1　The discursive construction of HK identity

In this chapter, I will tie together the key results that have arisen from the discursive analysis of the HK identity in the PAs pre-and post-transition. This task will be done in the light of the theoretical framework and the methodology of analysis described for the present investigation in Chapter 3. Some conclusive remarks and diachronic comparisons will be added from the analysis of the textual corpus of PAs.

This section summarises and comments on the results of the discourse analysis presented in the previous two chapters. First, the discussion of the results from the analysis of the pre-transitional sub-corpus shows the discursive strategies that shape and produce the discursive construction of HK identity, that is, the function and effect in constructing HK identity before the Transition. Then, the discussion of the results from the post-transitional sub-corpus offers the discursive construction of HK identity after the Transition. At last, a brief contrast and comparison of the discursive strategies is to follow.

### 6.1.1 Discursive construction of HK identity in the pre-transitional Policy Address

In relation to macro-strategies, a macro-content analysis of the PAs before the transition shows that sameness or uniqueness is constructed through the three major perspectives in the PA, common politics, common economy, and common culture, which create closeness and unity in HK. Through this commonness and unity, HK people were brought in-grouped. And this division between in-group and out-group at the same time backgrounds the differences of in-group and foregrounds the differences of out-group, and those that do not share this commonness are considered out-group. Significantly in the analysis, this sub-corpus of PA puts more emphasis on the discursive construction of common politics, compared with that in the post-transitional PA, and which may be explained that the British Colonial Government had tried to make changes to the original political systems, like the places of the Legislative Council and the age allowed for election, after the signing of the Joint Declaration and before the transition, which also became the contending point between China and Britain. This is also considered the political discursive strategy of constructing the differences between HK and China and alienating HK further from China.

The macro-strategies comprises, along with the content analysis, a title analysis and an analysis of some topics in the PA. The title analysis of the three PAs indicates the lack of continuation in the HK administration because of the coming transition. With the three titles, the British Colonial Government summoned its people to get prepared for the historic change which may imply that something urgent and threatening was confronting HK.

Besides the title analysis, an analysis of some of the important topics follows. The sections on the topic of relations with China discursively construct China as out-grouped by describing HK-China relations as cooperation which is lacking in mutual understanding. With China taken as out-grouped, the effect of this out-groupedness is brought forth by emphasizing the differences and distance between HK and China, displaying uncertainty of HK's future, presenting hindrances and tension among the relations of HK and China.

Moreover, the analysis on the topic of the positioning of HK shows that HK is assigned positive qualities of an economically-developed international center from whose situation China benefits in its development, which places HK on a giving end and China a receiving end. This topic emphasizes on the economic success and achievements of HK which at the same time mirrors the lack of success of China, in other words, to value HK's success is to devalue China.

Further, language is perceived as being important. In emphasizing HK's being international instead of being a colony of Britain, the official language in HK was English with HK a bi-lingual society of Cantonese and English. As is destined that HK is to be handed over to China, Chinese made its debut in HK laws and official documents in the late 1980s, but the competence of individuals in Chinese is totally neglected, which may be interpreted that the origin of the HK people as Chinese is totally neglected.

As is known, HK was a colony of Britain, but Britain refused to grant HK people full citizenship, which brought the nationality issue prominent to people living in HK. HK people were denied the right of abode in Britain by the British Authorities out of the consideration that the vast immigration from HK might influence Britain, so only those, a very small proportion of 50 000 heads of household who would not leave HK were rendered full British citizenship. The paradox lies in that the vast majority of HK people were ethnic Chinese but not Chinese citizens, holding a BNO Passport without enjoying the right of abode in Britain.

Summing up, the macro-strategies in the pre-transitional sub-corpus aim at constructing a HK in-group identity through the commonness of the three aspects of politics, economy and culture shared by the people of the whole community, with China as out-group though HK people's Chinese ethnicity is deliberately neglected. HK is depicted emphatically as an international centre instead of a city resided by ethnic Chinese. These macro-strategies take the semantic aspects of language into consideration, trying to answer the question of what is addressed in the PA to construct the in-group and out-group.

In relation to the micro-strategies, this research approached the pre-transitional sub-corpus in three levels of language use—lexical, sentential, and intertextual. The first level, lexical level, studies the referential strategies employed in this sub-corpus. The second level, sentential, provides an analysis of the rhetorical strategies that contribute to the discursive construction of HK identity. And the last level takes intertextuality as a discursive strategy in discursive identity construction. These micro-strategies are applied, based on the distinction of in-group and out-group by the macro-strategies, to attach certain values to the in-group and out-group.

Referential strategies are further divided into three types of reference, namely, personal reference, temporal reference and spatial reference. The first person plural pronoun "we" is analysed. Through the analysis of the use of "we", it is found that in this sub-corpus, "we" is used to include HK Government and HK people, exclusive of people outside HK which implies the distancing from the ethnic ancestor of the HK people, Chinese. As noted in previous studies (Wodak, 1999; Chilton, 2004), words with positive connotations will be linked to the in-group whereas words with negative connotations linked to the out-group and antonymous words help establish a dichotomy between "us" and "them". Another referential strategy is the employment of temporal references in this sub-corpus. Temporal references indicating the past are used to display the achievements of HK under the rule of Britain and British commitment to HK. Temporal references indicating the future signify a discontinuation in HK's future because of the transition which suggests uncertainty towards the future HKSAR Government and threat of failure brought forth by the transition. Of the temporal references, the time "1997" is used as a significant strategy to construct a negative image of China and a positive one of Britain. Spatial references play as the third sub-strategy. From the nomination of the three sides involved in HK's affairs, Britain, HK and China, a favorable relationship between Britain and HK is set up, with HK-China relationship a more international kind, which may not be favorable through placing an emphasis on HK's being international instead of a Chinese city. Results of the analysis of the referential strategies show that HK together with its colonial country, Britain are positively constructed, but China is referentially constructed as negative in this sub-corpus.

In addition, rhetorical strategies on sentential level are employed in this sub-corpus to assign HK positive qualities and China negative qualities. Allusion, as a rhetorical device, in this sub-corpus further detaches HK from China by alluding to some events in China and some contentious point during the period before transition. The PA chooses to express them implicitly for the reason that the British Colonial Government would not be responsible for referring to those negative events. Presupposition is another rhetorical device further devaluing China in several aspects—China's politics is too complex to get involved; China is an opponent of HK which imposes strain and stresses on the HK-China relations; China is an obstacle in the preparatory work of the transition; China is without democracy which surely constructs a derogatory Chinese image multi-dimensionally.

On super-sentential level, the strategy of intertextuality is analysed. The three sources of intertextuality are found to be proper names or familiar language usage, international elites, and the Basic Law. The general purpose for intertextuality in this corpus is to justify what the British Colonial Government has done, but which was severely protested by the Chinese Government. The Chinese Government is thus put on an unjustified end in the contest between China and Britain.

The micro-strategies on the three levels are taken into account in the analysis which aim at answering the question of what discursive strategies are involved and how they are employed in the pre-transitional sub-corpus to construct China as the out-group and simultaneously attach negative values to this out-group and thus alienate HK from China.

Finally, this analysis of the strategies, macro and micro, demonstrates the content or topics that are involved in the discursive construction of HK identity before the transition and how the strategies are employed in this construction. Results show that HK is discursive constructed to be positive—successful, democratic, open, free, etc. — and half in-grouped with Britain. In the PA, no complete integration into Britain is demonstrated because as a colonizer Britain would not take whole responsibility of HK and did not recognize HK people as British citizens and did not grant HK people full citizenship, as is illustrated in the sources of intertextuality— British Colonial HK Government seeks justification internationally and by international and universal stands. As is often quoted, HK was described as "a rock floating between two worlds", the world of far-off colonial Britain and China, the ancestor of 98% of the HK people. China is belittled and negatively represented as complex without democracy and freedom and forever on the contending end with HK. This analysis shows HK is distanced and alienated from China, thus HK identity is unique, HK citizen before the transition is constructed in the PA not to be British citizens as stipulated in the Common Law, but rather Hongkongers under the loose British rule. The following figure further illustrates this HK identity before the transition. The dotted line of Britain indicates its loose rule over HK.

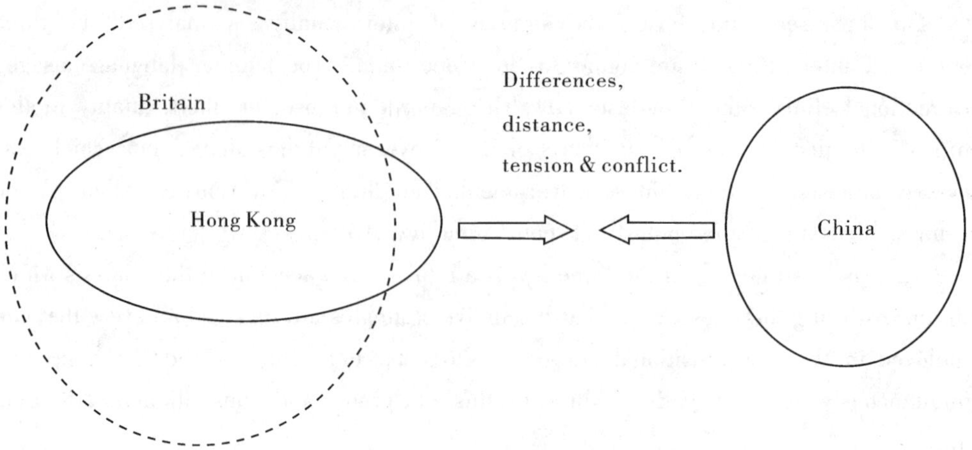


**Figure 1 HK Identity before the transition**

### 6.1.2 Discursive construction of HK identity in the post-transitional Policy Address

In this sub-corpus, both the macro-strategies and micro-strategies are examined. Macro-strategies are assigned the function of answering the question of what aspects or content or topics are addressed in contribution to the discursive identity construction, while micro-strategies are to answer the question of how the identity is discursively constructed through the use of different means of linguistic strategies. Thus, macro-strategies are roughly on the semantic level, while the micro-strategies roughly on the pragmatic level.

In relation to the macro-strategies in the post-transitional PA, as employed in the pre-transitional sub-corpus, the three aspects of politics, economy and culture are involved in each PA, which create closeness and unity in HK. Through this closeness and unity, HK people are brought into in-group. And this division between in-group and out-group at the same time backgrounds the differences of in-group and foregrounds the differences of out-group, and those that do not share this commonness are considered out-group. At this point, only HK people are considered in-grouped, with people outside HK out-grouped. The content analysis shows that the HKSAR Government places much emphasis on its economy, and contributes less to its politics. These results may be interpreted from two aspects. On the one hand, immediately after the transition, HK experienced the Asian financial turmoil which led to the fact that the core work of the

HKSAR Government was transferred to economic development. On the other hand, since HK is now identifying with "One Country, Two System" "Hong Kong people ruling Hong Kong", and "the present political systems will remain unchanged 50 years", no revision to the political systems is allowed and no development is this respect is necessary. Hence, these three aspects in the post-transitional PA are involved in the discursive identity construction which exclude people outside HK and unify people in HK.

Following the content analysis is a topic analysis of the titles as well as some topics that are regarded critical to the identity construction in this sub-corpus. Altogether in the eleven PAs, we have eight PAs that are entitled. With these eight titles, besides constructing sameness, commonness and uniqueness of HK, the PAs also convey the government's administration principles in different years which are taken as shared experience of HK people and help with the identity construction.

In line with the topic analysis, some topics are reviewed that play an important role in the discursive construction of HK identity, of which "relations with China" was placed in the first place because the working definition of identity in the present study is defined as the HK-China relations. After 1997, the HKSAR Government establishes a new type of relation with China by pinpointing the sameness in common interests shared by HK and China. In the relations between HK and China, this sub-corpus of PA stresses the dependence of HK on China and due to such a fact, HK should shoulder the responsibility in the development of the country. And in the process of establishing a favorable relation with China, HK should avoid some sensitive issues that might cause misunderstanding or displeasure on the Chinese side. Thus it can be inferred that the HKSAR Government would subordinate HK to China and thus gain more dependence.

The topic of "positioning of HK" is of most importance in that the way to position HK is the way to identify HK people. In this sub-corpus, HK is placed a region attached to China, from whose relationship HK is on the beneficial side by emphasizing the achievements and success of the open-and-reform policy of China. It is a way of identifying with China by evaluating China positively. Hence the analysis of this topic embodies the HKSAR Government's integration into China.

As illustrated by Joseph's (2004), collective identities are manifested primarily through the shared language, so the language policies in HK may be significant in their identity construction. After the transition, the promotion of Putonghua, the Chinese official language, as the teaching language went through an n-shaped process of change. Because of the pressure from HK society that HK should be internationally competitive with a certain proficiency of English and also Chinese Government's support of English as the teaching language, the HKSAR Government at last gave up the benchmark of Putonghua in HK. But from such a series of events, it is evident in showing the HKSAR Government's determination to incorporate into mainland China. But furthermore what we can infer should be that policies without support of its people will cause protest and be doomed in failure.

The topic of national education might be impossible before the transition or even right after the transition. The interpretation of its first appearance only in the recent two years may be that the HKSAR Government would not make changes to the old system to keep confidence in HK (Flowerdew, 2002). From this topic, what we can detect is the kind of ideology permeation—Chinese people should devote to China. This is to identify with the interests or values in China, or in other words, a kind of brainwash to remove the memory of colonial administration.

Summing up, the macro-strategies in the post-transitional sub-corpus aim at setting up a favorable relationship with China and thus identifying with China's success and values, which corresponds to the working definition of identity in the present research that identity—idea of aligning oneself to certain interests, values, beliefs of social groups (Ivanic, 1998) and also HK identity is termed in its relations with China. Hence, what can be concluded from the analysis of the macro-strategies in the sub-corpus of the post-transitional PA is that China is constructed in-grouped, and HK people are Chinese though they possess their uniqueness.

The analysis of the micro-strategies in this sub-corpus unfolds in the way of that in the sub-corpus of the pre-transitional PA. This research approaches the post-transitional sub-corpus in three levels of language use—lexical, sentential, and intertextual. The first level, lexical level, studies the three referential sub-strategies employed in this sub-corpus. The second level, sentential, provides an analysis of the rhetorical devices that contribute to the discursive construction of HK identity. And the last level takes intertextuality as a discursive strategy in discursive identity construction. These micro-strategies are applied, based on the distinction of in-group and out-group by the macro-strategies, to attach certain values to the in-group and out-group.

Referential strategies are analysed in three categories. The first person plural "we" is studied as a personal referential strategy. In this sub-corpus, though "we" is used mostly to include the HKSAR Government and people in HK, the significant discovery is that "we" is sometimes used as a strategy to include Chinese people and thus to place Chinese people or China in-grouped. Thus it can be inferred that words with positive connotations would be linked with this in-group. Another type of references, temporal references, is used to set up the common history and common future of HK. In this sub-corpus, near or far future is discursively set up more prominent than the past history, which seems to be something that the HKSAR Government would not mention or is unwilling to touch upon. Further, the year 1997 is significant in this sub-corpus that it indicates a historic change and brings a new life to the HK people and which makes HK people finally become their own master (2005PA) and in which year "HK has finally broken free from the psychological constraints brought about by the colonial era". (1997PA) Moreover it should be the time heartedly welcomed by the HKSAR Government because its being was due to the transition in that year. Here lies the significance of the temporal reference of "1997". The last type of references is the spatial references. The references indicating China are of positive connotation and much emotional. References indicating HK demonstrate HK's Chineseness and references of Britain are totally absent in this sub-corpus. Traces can be found concerning the previous colonial country in phrases like "colonial administration" or "colonial rule" which suggest something completely negative. All in all, the referential strategies employed in this sub-corpus dedicate to the construction of a positive China and a negative colonial past.

Moreover, another micro-strategy, rhetorical strategy comprising of the rhetorical devices of allusion and presupposition, is discovered in this sub-corpus. Allusion in this sub-corpus tries to allude to some events that are negative to China instead of expressing it explicitly. In so doing, the seriousness of such negative events is alleviated in public opinion. Presupposition is another rhetorical device deployed to set up discursively a positive China. In this sub-corpus, the five expositions of presupposition given in the previous chapter all are devoted to the idea that China is greatly credited for what HK is enjoying now—success, achievements, democracy, freedom, etc., thus an image of a helpful and great motherland is created. Hereby, rhetorical devices are proved essential to the discursive construction of an identity.

Intertextuality, as a discursive micro-strategy above the sentential level, also contributes to a HK identity integrating into China. Of the three sources of intertextuality, two originate from the Chinese side, which indicate that the HKSAR Government turns to the Chinese Central Government for lawfulness and authoritativeness of what is stated in the PA, and which further shows the high identification with Chinese values and opinions, at least of the Chinese Government or the Chinese leaders.

The micro-strategies on the three levels of lexical, sentential and textual, are taken into account in the analysis which aim at answering the question of what discursive strategies are involved and how they are employed in the post-transitional sub-corpus to construct China as in-grouped and simultaneously attach positive values and identification to this in-group and thus align HK with China.

In conclusion, this analysis of the strategies, macro and micro, demonstrates the content or topics that are involved in the discursive construction of HK identity after the transition and how the pragmatic strategies are employed in this construction. Results show that HK is discursive constructed to be positive—successful, democratic, open, free, etc. — and this positive image of HK is due to the its incorporation into China and thus China is positively represented successful and helpful to HK. However, HK people are still not equal to Mainland Chinese for they keep their own political systems that are different from Mainland China thus own their own inside commonness and unity. The distinction between Hongkongese and Chinese are demonstrated in the government's PA but more importantly the inclination of integration is sharp and the yearning for integration is evident. In this way, this analysis shows HK is aligned with and attached to China, thus HK identity is unique in that it has its unique politics, economy and culture not shared with Mainland China, which is in line with the Fung's (2008) "HK identities are different from Mainland Chinese identities" . But in a more important sense, HK people are Chinese, as illustrated in the following figure.

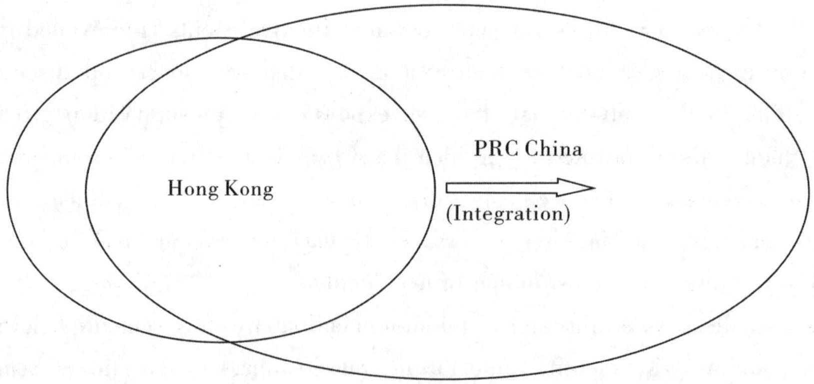


**Figure 2 HK identity after the transition**

## 6.2 A theoretical discussion of the discursive construction of identity

In contrast to other paradigms in discourse analysis, CDA would require a theorization and description of both the social processes and structures which give rise to the production of a text, and of the social structures and processes within which individuals or groups as social historical subjects, create meanings in their interaction with texts (Fairclough & Kress, 1993). Consequently, the three concepts figure indispensably in all CDA: the concept of power, the concept of history, and the concept of ideology (Wodak, 2001). Thus the discursive HK identity construction will be discussed along these three dimensions which are considered to be interrelated to each other.

### 6.2.1 The concept of power

The constant unity of language and other social matters ensure that language is entwined in social power in a number of ways: language indexes power, expresses power, is involved where there is contention over and a challenge to power.

For CDA, language is not powerful on its own—it gains power by the use powerful people make of it (Wodak, 2001). Those who have greater social power have greater social access to socially valued resources of dominant discourse. In our present research, HK governments' PA is delivered by the HK Governor before the transition or the CE of the HKSAR Government, who are the highest official in this community and hence their speeches are highly influential and of most power in nature. Thus, the deliverer of the PA determines the powerfulness of this discourse.

Language is also a means of expressing its manipulative power. In the term critical discourse analysis, "critique" is essentially making visible the interconnectedness of things (Fairclough, 1985). In Fairclough's words, "in human matters, interconnections and chains of cause and effect may be distorted out of vision". In Flowerdew's (1998) words, a situation is created where a particular state of affairs is judged to be perfectly normal and acceptable. Manipulation may be conceptualized in that discourse becomes naturalized and ideological element is no longer apparent. Thus it is a critical analyst's job to uncover the manipulativeness of a discourse. In our present analysis of the discursive construction of HK identities, it is evident that the two HK governments' PA sub-corpora constructed two distinct identities by means of nearly the same strategies. Without an in-depth analysis, it would be uneasy to discover the manipulation of the discourse because the two processes of the categorization of in-group and the values attached to the in-group/out-group differ vastly in the two sub-corpora in the present research. The way of grouping or the HK-China relationship was naturalized by continually repeating this ideology, in which a new ideology is taken as natural and acceptable and thus a new identity is constructed. Thus, we can see the power of a discourse also lies in its power of manipulation through a process of naturalization.

Power does not derive from language, but language can be used to challenge power, to subvert it, to alter distributions of power in the short or long term. Language provides a finely articulated means for differences in power in social hierarchical structures. Power is bi-directional. It is very rare for a text to be the work of any one person. In texts discursive differences are negotiated; they are governed by differences in power which are themselves in part encoded in the determined way by discourse. Therefore texts are often sites of struggle in that they show traces of differing discourses and ideologies contending and struggling for dominance (van Dijk, 1997). As in our intertextual analysis, the PA before the transition tends to seek authoritativeness from some international standard, while the post-transitional PA seeks authoritativeness by means of intertextualizing the words from Mainland China. Thus it is self-evident that different powers play a role in the PA's construction of HK identities.

Furthermore, the power in discourse has its effectiveness for a given period of time. The constructive power and the manipulative power in discourse disfunction when the administration is no longer in power. As the sovereignty of HK was transferred from Britain to China on July 1st, 1997, the PA of the British Colonial HK Government could no longer exert its influence. This is the historicality of discourse and the historical power in discourse.

### 6.2.2 The concept of ideology

Ideology is the basis of knowledge, knowledge that is shared by the community linguistically and culturally (van Dijk, 1997). As the basis of knowledge, ideologies are more like underlying principles, social "cognitions" which influence, shape and form knowledge, beliefs and attitudes shared by that community (van Dijk, 1997). Ideologies are developed by dominant groups in order to legitimate their domination (van Dijk, 1997). In other words, ideologies help structure and make knowledge, common beliefs or social attitudes "reasonable and natural", and persuade the dominated groups to take such social relation for granted. According to van Dijk (1997), without cognitive analysis, these studies "can not reveal how societal structure influences discourse structure, and how then these structures in turn are enacted, legitimised, instituted, and confirmed or challenged by text".

Through complex and usually long-term processes of socialization and other forms of social information processing, ideologies are gradually acquired by members of a group or culture. As systems of principles that organize social cognitions, ideologies are assumed to control, through the minds of the members, the social reproduction of the group. Ideologies mentally represent the basic social characteristics of a group, such as their identities, tasks, goals, norms, values, positions and resources. Since ideologies are usually self-serving, it would seem that they are organized by these group-schemata. The structures of ideologies also suggest that such representations are often articulated along with an "us" versus "them" dimension, in which speakers of one group will generally tend to present themselves or their own group in positive terms, and other groups in negative terms (van Dijk, 2006). Thus, any property of discourse that expresses, establishes, confirms or emphasizes a selfinterested group opinion, perspective or position, especially in a broader socio-political context of social struggle, is a candidate for special attention in such an ideological analysis. Such discourse structures usually have the social function of legitimating dominance or justifying concrete actions of power abused by the elites. The specific group tends to present the relations between themselves and the others essentially in terms of "us" versus "them", in which we are associated with positive properties and they are associated with negative properties. Such ideologies of groups and group relations are constructed by a group-based selection of relevant social values. In our present research, these polarized ideologies demonstrate themselves in the grouping of the concept of "Hong Kong people". In the pre-transitional PA, the British Colonial HK Government tends to put Mainland China on the opposite side of HK and thus outgroup China. Whereas in the post-transitional PA of the HKSAR Government tends to categorize Mainland China as in-grouped with HK. After the grouping of certain community, different values are attached to different groups, with positive values to the in-group and negative values to the out-group. Through these two steps, certain relations between in-group and out-group are represented and reproduced. In a word, through the construction of certain ideologies, discourse becomes manipulative covertly.

Generally though, ideologies more specifically control evaluative beliefs, that is, social opinions shared by the members of a group. Ideologies are very specific basic frameworks of social cognition, with specific internal structures, and specific cognitive and social functions. Furthermore, they are social, for they are essentially shared by groups and acquired, used, and changed by people as group members in social situations and institutions, often in situations of conflicting interests between social formations (Eagleton, 1991). However, ideologies are not restricted to dominant groups. Oppositional or dominated groups also share ideologies. Thus, in order that their discourse accepted and their administration supported, the dominating group has to take the ideologies of the dominated groups into consideration in their discourse. As has been mentioned in 4. 2. 5, in order to maintain the confidence on the part of HK people that there would be little change from the old system, the HKSAR government hasn't put forward the topic of "national education" in the first ten years after the 1997 transition. In sum, though PA is the sole work of the government, the dominant group, we can identify contending ideologies in the same discourse through our analysis.

The examination of this social cultural change and change of discourse is part of a critical discourse analysis. Such a public discourse involves advocacy of social practices, and through a shift of public discourse practices the boundary between the public and private social life can be blurred: what is in the public domain will affect the discourse of private social life. When people are exposed repeatedly to the actions and directions of the Government and the media coverage, it may result in changes in their ideologies. It is not our research focus whether the HK people have changed their ideologies of their identities, but it is our interest to uncover the covertness of manipulation in our present data of the HK governments' PA. The manipulation in discourses at the same time manipulates ideology construction, which remains to be covert compared with the socio-political change. In the analytical framework of our present research, superficially, the PAs employ nearly the same strategies before and after the socio-political change of the 1997 transition, while the identities, hence ideologies, constructed in the PA are sharply in contrast before and after the transition. Thus we can draw that overt socio-political change results in covert discourse changes and in turn ideology changes. This then confirms what van Dijk (1997) asserted: "The more powerful groups can manipulate the ideologies of other subordinate groups through twisting information in the campaign, through its control over the media, and through managing the possible opposition into support." Ideologies can be discursively constructed, transformed and manipulated.

### 6.2.3 The concept of history

Discourse is historical, both synchronically and diachronically.

Discourse constitutes and is constituted by reality (Fairclough, 1989). Synchronically, the discourse of PA cannot be produced without the specific context, neither can it be understood or interpreted without taking the context into consideration and without understanding the embedded culture and ideologies. Diachronically, to understand the discourse we should relate the PA to the past. Readers of the PA would not easily understand the far-reaching influence of the legislation of Article 23 in the BL if the PA were not related to the past. Thus through history we may better interpret the PA, whereas through the PA we may better penetrate the identity construction as well as ideology construction in the PA.

Identity is not only discursively constructed, it covaries with socio-political change. To understand the social interaction and implications, according to Fairclough (1989, 1992), one needs to look at the relationship between cultural change and discursive change. In this case, every language user makes a small contribution to transforming society and culture, and also to reproducing power relations (van Dijk, 1997). Government having easy access to discourse over power in turns represents and is represented by the society. Cultural political change may be perceived in the manifestation of this shift in discourse and identity.

In conclusion, discourse is the product of power and is highly ideological and historical, and the same case is with identity and identity construction. Through this discussion, the interrelations and interactions of the three concepts, namely power, ideology and historicality in discourse are revealed.

## 6.3 A summary

Starting with a retrospection of the analysis of the identity construction in the two HK governments' PA in the previous two chapters, Chapter 4 and Chapter 5, this chapter further discusses the discursive construction of the two distinct HK identities pre- and post-transition through the application of the various discursive strategies. The conclusion is reached that in the PA before transition, HK people were not simply British citizens in HK, but HK people under the rule of Britain, and that after transition, HK people are discursively constructed as Chinese Hongkongers in the

PA. Then follows a discussion of the discursive construction of identity in CDA, particularly with concepts of power, ideology and historicality which are highly interrelated in the discursive identity construction. This discussion of the present chapter highly echoes the theories in CDA.

# Chapter 7 Discursive Construction of HK Identities

## 7.1 Introduction

The aim of the present study has been to carry a comparative analysis of the discursive strategies in the construction of HK identity in two sub-corpora of HK governments' PAs. As a frequently visited socio-linguistic topic which is often lack of systematicity, HK identity in discourse needs a more comprehensive and in-depth study and a coherently operational and interdisciplinary framework. In agreement with this demand, the present research has attempted to reveal the complexity of HK identity in the particular genre of PA by generating an operational and interdisciplinary framework based on Wodak's (1999) discourse-historic approach. This framework is able to take into account the linguistic, social, cultural, political factors. In accordance with this framework, the present study has provided a full picture of the two distinct HK identities discursively constructed in the two HK governments' PAs by analyzing and discussing in detail the discursive strategies that are employed in the PAs.

This chapter commences with a brief summary of the major findings in the previous chapters followed by the contributions and theoretical implications of this study. Then the limitations of this study are pointed out with the purpose of achieving some possible improvements in such a study. Finally some recommendations for future research are made.

## 7.2 Major findings, theoretical contributions and implications

### 7.2.1 Major findings

Based on the analytical framework and the theoretical approach worked out previously, this research processed the data of the HK governments' PAs in order to solve the problem of the discursive construction of the two HK identities pre-vs. post-transition. Findings from the present research can be concluded as follows:

(1) The transition of sovereignty of HK from Britain to China that took place in 1997 brought forth the transition of HK identity. Before the transition, the British Colonial HK Government alienates HK from China, while after the transition, the HKSAR Government aligns HK with China's values, interests, standard, etc.

(2) Before the transition, HK people were defined in their Common Law as "British citizens in HK" . However through our research, we have found in the PA before 1997, HK people are not constructed as defined in the Common Law. Though HK people living in HK before 1997 were 95% ethnic Chinese, they are emphasized on their uniqueness of being Hongkongese and the British rule over HK is given less attention. Instead, the pre-transitional PA focuses more the internationalness of HK identity.

(3) After the transition, the uniqueness of HK is still foregrounded in order to construct an image of a successful and prosperous HK. Besides this uniqueness, the PA after 1997 displays a yearning for integration into Mainland China. Therefore, HK identity in the HKSAR Government's PA is constructed as Chinese Hongkongers with its Chineseness being emphasized.

(4) The contrast in the two discursively constructed identities of HK people pre- and post-transition results from the socio-political change of the transition, for which a decisive factor that influences the HK identities is the HK-China relationship. In other words, when China is out-grouped in the HK government's PA, HK people are alienated from China by its government; and when China is in-grouped in the HK government's PA, HK people are aligned with China by its government. The administrative concept is intertextualized as the common goal of the community of HK through the construction of the HK identity.

(5) Before the transition, in order to construct a negative China's image, the negative side of China is foregrounded with China's positiveness backgrounded. While in the same way, after the transition, in order to integrate into China and construct an in-grouped China, the negative side of China is minified with its positiveness magnified.

### 7.2.2 Theoretical contributions and implications

As has been reviewed in Chapter 2, Wodak (1999) puts forward an analytical framework for the study of identity in sociolinguistics which elaborates four types of strategies. At the same time, she points out that in political discourse, the strategy of construction is mostly used. In this research and basing on Wodak's (1999) framework, the present researcher works out a framework for the discursive construction of identity in political discourse. In analysing the discursive construction of an identity, the indispensable points are what topics are addressed and how to employ linguistic devices, the former constituting the macro-strategies in our present framework and the latter the micro-strategies. On a second layer of this present framework, macro-strategies, or the content of the discourse, can be analysed in the concerned aspects and the involved topics; micro-strategies, or the linguistic means, can be analysed on three levels—lexical, sentential and textual. Such an analytical framework provides an alternative analytical framework in the study of identity that has been proved to work in this research.

Significance of this study lies in the mapping of the micro-level linguistic properties of a communicative act onto macro-level phenomena in the political realm that leads to a better understanding of the functionality of these linguistic properties in political discourse. It is important to understand that the analytical framework, together with the discursive strategies, that has been developed in the present study is one step further on Wodak's (1999) framework and could be implemented in other discourse communities and in other languages for the study of identity construction in political discourse. The integration of a linguistic and non-linguistic framework for discourse analysis may provide a way for examining writers' discursive practices in other socio-cultural contexts, as Wodak (2006) has noted, "the theoretical constructions of discourse which CDA tries to operationalize can come from various disciplines, and the concept of 'operationalization' entails working in a transdisciplinary way where the logic of one discipline (for example, sociology) can be 'put to work' in the development of another (for example, linguistics)". Furthermore, the framework in the present research could be extended to similar research fields like international relationship. And this research to some extent enriches the identity theories and discursive construction of identity in sociolinguistics and also contributes to CDA.

Based on this research on the discursive construction of HK identity and also the transfer of HK identity, some theoretical implications can be identified as follows:

(1) The two sub-corpora of PA before transition and after transition display the same types of strategies, but two HK identities are constructed, with one alienating

from China in the pre-transitional PA and another aligning with China in the post-transitional PA, which highly corresponds with that of van Dijk (1997) —"language is highly manipulative" in its application of the same types of strategies with different identities constructed.

(2) Identity is largely ideological. As van Dijk (1997) puts it, ideologies are polarized in which the in-group or we is often constructed to be positive and the out-group or they is often constructed as negative. Discourse is manipulative because ideology is manipulable, thus, the discursive construction of an identity can be highly manipulated.

(3) From this research, we have this inter-relationship—socio-political change influences community identity which in turn has impact on language use. Socio-political change may be abrupt and overt, but language change may be gradual and covert.

(4) CDA is an effective approach to the socio-linguistic study of identity. Identity is a complex concept and subject to socio-political changes, and CDA is an interdisciplinary approach integrating social, political, cultural and linguistic factors. Therefore the study of discursively constructed identity may be and should be done in the framework of CDA.

(5) The power of discourse can be illustrated both in the powerful people who address it and the highly manipulative nature of a discourse, that discourse are ideological, and that discourse, power and ideology are historical.

6) Discourse is the contending field of different forces with different voices out of different interests.

## 7.3 Limitations of this study

Although the present study has revealed, to a certain degree, the full complexity of HK identity by analyzing the discursive macro- and micro-strategies in the two HK governments' PA, there are still certain limitations owing to the scantiness of relevant literature and the pressure of research time.

The most obvious limitation of the study is that some of the data analyses lack strong empirical support. Although the whole research is carried out with the alertness of reducing and avoiding subjectivity, disputes may still come forth due to the theory of CDA that has been criticized by Widdowson (1995) that "in the first place it is prejudiced on the basis of some ideological commitment, and then it selects for analysis such texts as will support the preferred interpretation". Fairclough (1996), in reply to this criticism, points out that CDA, unlike most other approaches, is always explicit about its own position and commitment. It is impossible to achieve a universal understanding for any linguistic phenomenon and it is also unlikely to cater for all tastes in any data analysis.

Another weak point of the study is, for pressure of research time available, the limited scope of data examined for the analysis. Although much effort has been devoted to data collection in the present study, further improvements are still desired. For example, it would have been better if we had had access to the HK people's attitude to their identity and their own identification because such a study on the impact of the PA on the public and investigating its reception, could probably achieve more fruitful findings and could make the sketched picture of HK identity more comprehensive and neutral.

Last but not least, the present study lacks exhaustiveness to certain extent. It is especially the case with Chapter 5, which reveals the micro-strategies in the PA, and the findings of which are by no means exhaustive. After all, the dynamic nature of politics and identity makes it too challenging, if not impossible, to exhaust all the strategies in the PA because new PAs keep emerging yearly and new political situation keeps changing. As the present author lives outside HK, lack of exhaustiveness in the interpretation is not avoidable.

## 7.4 Suggestions for future research

Up to now, a detailed study on the discursively constructed HK identity in the two governments' PAs has been presented; however, such a contrastive study is but an initial attempt in the specific genre of PA since many issues are still open to future endeavours.

First of all, although the present study analysed 22 texts of PA, further research could be carried out to include more political discourses besides PA, such as political interviews, election campaigns, etc., which can be found in HK during this 23 years. Larger corpora could be established to examine the different tendencies of common language use in texts. Furthermore, in the present study what is contrasted are the two periods of the time right before the transition and after, but further research may set another earlier period when the JD was not signed and when sovereignty of HK was not decided to hand over to China, which might bring broader differences in the discursively constructed HK identity.

The present research has been based on the HK data, but HK identity discursively constructed is by no means restricted to HK; rather HK problem involved three parties of China, Britain and HK. Therefore, we may conduct some similar researches on the data collected outside HK, such as documents in British Government or Chinese Government on HK problems. We may also carry out some comparative studies on the political discourse in China, Britain and HK.

Since the present study analysed only the voice of the HK governments, the scope of research should be extended so as to include the voice of the public. For example, future study of HK identity could be done through surveys in HK people which may be considered to be an ethnographical procedure and which could gain insights into the core values and beliefs of the practices of the community. More revealing significance could be expected through a survey and data analyzing which aim to make visible the beliefs and practices of members of this unique culture and community. A survey in the HK public, in other words, may provide thicker pictures of the problem of identity. That is, it could illustrate the scenes behind pure linguistic features found in discourse analysis.

In conclusion, the above-mentioned three approaches to extend this research are not conclusive or exhaustive. They simply highlight some of the analytical approaches or fields that could be explored from different aspects. Different approaches have strengths and weaknesses in contributing to the knowledge of HK identity. The specific knowledge generated by any one approach or any one framework is only one part of the elephant. It may, therefore, be concluded that identity studies in discourse could be greatly enhanced by employing a multi-dimensional view of analysis which has an interest in the integration of different research methodologies and frameworks for analyzing discourses and practices in various professional, institutional and social domains. In a word, identity will continue to be a fascinating research topic in sociolinguistics and it is right there waiting for further inquiries.

# References


[1] Abraham, T. 2002. Lack of choice behind weakness in Tung support. South China morning post. Apr. 7.

[2] Ackbar, A. 1997. Other histories, other politics. Public culture, 9 (3): 293 – 313.

[3] Ainsorth, S. & Hardy, C. 2004. Critical discourse analysis and identity: Why bother? Critical discourse studies, 1 (2): 225 – 259.

[4] Allen, G. 2000. Intertextuality. London: Routledge.

[5] Anderson, B. 1983. Imagined communities: Reflections on the origins and spread of nationalism. London: Verso.

[6] Asp, K. 1986. Mäktiga massmedier: Studier i politisk pinionsbildning [Powerful mass media: studies in political opinion-formation] . Stockholm: Akademilitteratur.

[7] Austin, J. L. 1961. Philosophical Papers. Oxford: Clarendon Press.

[8] Authier-Revus J. , Lala M-Ch. (éd. ) 2002. Figures d'ajout: phrase, texte, écriture. Presses Sorbonne nouvelle.

[9] Bakhtin, M. 1981. The dialogic imagination. Austin: University of Texas Press.

[10] Bakhtin, M. 1986. Speech genres and other late essays. Austin: University of Texas Press.

[11] Baker, C. 1983. A microanalysis of the non-manual components of questions in American sign language. In P. Siple (ed.), Understanding language through sign language research. New York: Academic Press.

[12] Bazerman, C. 1993. Foreword to professional communication: The social perspective. London: Sage.

[13] Baynham, M. 1999. Double-voicing and the scholarly " I ": On incorporating the words of others in academic discourse. Text, 19 (4):

485 – 504.

[14] Bazerman, C. 2004. Intertextuality: How texts rely on other texts. In C. Bazerman & P. Prior (eds.), What writing does and how it does it: An introduction to analyzing texts and textual practices. Mahwah, New Jersey: Erlbaum.

[15] Beard, A. 2000. The language of politics. London: Routledge.

[16] Beaugrande, R. 1997. New foundations for a science of text and discourse. Norwood, New Jersey: Ablex.

[17] Ben-Porat, Z. 1976. The poetics of literary allusion. A journal for descriptive poetics and theory of literature, 1: 105 – 108.

[18] Bell, A. & Garret, P. (eds.) . 1998. Approaches to media discourse. Oxford: Blackwell.

[19] Berelson, B. 1952. Content analysis in communication research. New York : Free Press.

[20] Berger, P. L. & Luckman, T. 1967. The social construction of reality. London: Doubleday.

[21] Bhahba, H. 1994. Location of culture. London: Routledge.

[22] Bhatia, V. K. 1993. Analyzing genre: Language use in professional settings. London: Longman.

[23] Bhatia, V. K. 1995. Genre-mixing in professional communication: The case of 'private intentions' vs. 'socially recognized purposes' . In P. Bruthiaux, T. Boswood & B. Bertha (eds.), Explorations in English for professional communication. Hong Kong: City University of Hong Kong.

[24] Bhatia, V. K. 2001. The power and politics of genre. In A. Burns & C. Coffin (eds.), Analysing English in a global context: A Reader. London, New York: Routledge.

[25] Bhatia, V. K. 1997. Democratizing decision making: A study of public discourse in Hong Kong. Journal of pragmatics, 28: 515 – 532.

[26] Bhatia, V. K. 2004. Worlds of written discourse. London, New York: Continuum.

[27] Biber, D. & Finegan, E. (eds.) 1994. Sociolinguistic perspectives on register. New York: Oxford University Press.

[28] Billig, M. 2003. Political rhetoric. In L. Huddy, R. Jervis & D. O. Sears (eds.), Oxford handbook of political psychology. New York: Oxford University Press.

[29] Blommaert, J. & Verschueren, J. 1998. Debating diversity: Analysing the discourse of tolerance. London, New York: Routledge.

[30] Blommaert, J. 2005. Discourse, a critical introduction. Cambridge: Cambridge University Press.

[31] Blomert, R., H. Kuzmics & A. Treibel. 1993. Transformationen des Wir-Gefuhls: Studien zum nationalen Habitus. Frankfurt a. M.

[32] Bourdieu, P. 1994. In other words: Essays towards a reflexive sociology. Cambridge: Cambridge University Press.

[33] Boyd-Barrett, O. 1994. Language and media: A question of convergence. In D. Graddol & O. Boyd-Barrett (eds.), Media texts: Authors and readers. Clevendon: Multilingual Matters Ltd.

[34] Bradford, R. 1997. Stylistics. London: Routledge.

[35] Brenneis, D. 1986. Shared territory: Audience, indirection and meaning. Text, 6 (3): 339 -347.

[36] Brown, G. & Yule, G. 1983. Discourse analysis. Cambridge: Cambridge University Press.

[37] Burr, V. 2003. Social constructionism (second edition). New York: Routledge.

[38] Butt, D., Lukin, A. & Matthiessen, C. 2004. Grammar—The first covert operation of war. Discourse and society, 15 (2 -3): 267 -290.

[39] Caldas-Coulthard, C. R. 1999. Women who pay for sex and enjoy it: Transgression versus morality in women's magazines. In Jaworski, A. & Coupland, N. (eds.), The discourse reader. London: Routledge.

[40] Cap, P. 2002. Explorations in political discourse: Methodological and critical perspectives. Frankfurt, Main: Lang.

[41] Chan, E. 2002. Beyond pedagogy: Language and identity in post-colonial Hong Kong. British journal of sociology of education, 23 (2): 271 -285.

[42] Chandler, D. 2005. Semiotics for beginners. Retrieved March 10, 2007, from University of Wales Web site: http://www.aber.ac.uk/media/Documents/S4B/sem02.html.

[43] Chen J. C. & Smith, R. A. 1997. Experimental design and analysis in understanding machining mechanisms. Journal of industrial technology, 13 (3): 15 -19.

[44] Cheng, J. 1984. The future of Hong Kong. The Australian journal of Chinese affairs, 12 (7): 113 -142.

[45] Cheng, T. 1997. Tung's first 100 days establishes his credibility. Hong Kong Standard.

[46] Chilton, P. 2004. Analysing political discourse: Theory and practice. London: Routledge.

[47] Chouliaraki, L. & Fairclough, N. 1999. Discourse in late modernity: Rethinking critical discourse analysis. Edinburgh: Edinburgh University Press.

[48] Cicourel, A V. 1969. Generative semantics and the structure of social interaction. Rome: Luigisturzo Institute.

[49] Collins, J. 1989. Uncommon cultures: Popular culture and post modernism. New York: Routledge.

[50] Coombs, J. H. 1984. Allusion defined and explained. Poetics, 13: 477 –488.

[51] Coupland, N. & Nussbaum, J. 1993. Discourse and lifespan identity. Newbury Park: Sage.

[52] Coulthard, M (ed) . 1994. Advances in written text analysis. London, New York: Routledge.

[53] Culler, J. 1981. The pursuit of signs: Semiotics, literature, deconstruction. London: Routledge & Kegan Paul.

[54] Danet, B. 1984. "Intoduction" . Text: An interdisciplinary journal for the study of discourse, 4: 1 –8.

[55] de Fina, A. 2006. Group identity, narrative, and self-representations. In A. de Fina, D. Schiffrin, & M. Bamberg (eds.), Discourse and identity. Cambridge: Cambridge University Press.

[56] Devitt, M. 1991. Realism and truth. Princeton: Princeton University Press.

[57] Dillard, J. P. & Pfau, M. 2002. The persuasion handbook: developments in theory and practice. Thousand Oaks, CA: Sage.

[58] Dra. E. H. 2006. The discursive construction of Gibraltarian identity in the printed press. Unpublished PhD. Dissertation. Retrieved from: http: // hera. ugr. es/tesisugr/16077507. pdf.

[59] Duranti, A. & Goodwin, C. (eds.) 1992. Rethinking context: Language as an interactive phenomenon. Cambridge: Cambridge University Press.

[60] Eagleton, T. 1991. Ideology: An introduction. London: Grant McIntyre.

[61] Elias, H. M. 1992. Commentary: Abuse of the child sexual abuse accommodation syndrome. Journal of childhood sexual abuse, 1: 169 –171.

[62] Fairclough, N. 1985. Critical and descriptive goals in discourse analysis. Journal of pragmatics, 9: 739 - 763.
[63] Fairclough, N. 1989. Language and power. London: Longman.
[64] Fairclough, N. 1992a. Discourse and social change. Cambridge: Polity Press.
[65] Fairclough, N. (ed.) 1992b. Critical language awareness. London: Longman.
[66] Fairclough, N. 1993. Critical discourse analysis and the marketization of public discourse: The universities. Discourse and society, 4 (2): 68 - 133.
[67] Fairclough, N. 1995a. Critical discourse analysis. London: Longman.
[68] Fairclough, N. 1995b. Media discourse. London: Edward Arnold.
[69] Fairclough, N. 1996. A Reply to Henry Widdowson's discourse analysis: A critical view. Language and literature, 5 (1): 49 - 56.
[70] Fairclough, N. 1998. Political discourse in the media: An analytical framework. In Bell, A & Garrett, P (eds.), Approaches to media discourse. Oxford: Blackwell.
[71] Fairclough, N. 2000. Discourse, social theory and social research: The discourse of welfare reform. Journal of sociolinguistics, 4 (2): 163 - 195.
[72] Fairclough, N. 2001. The discourse of new labor: Critical discourse analysis. In Wetherall, M., Taylor, S. & Yates, S. (eds.), Discourse as data: A guide for analysis. London: Sage/Open University.
[73] Fairclough, N. 2003. Analysing discourse: Text analysis for social research. London: Routledge.
[74] Fairclough, N. & Kress, G. 1993. Critical discourse analysis. Unpublished manuscript.
[75] Fairclough, N. & Wodak, R. 1997. Critical discourse analysis. In van Dijk, T. (ed.), Discourse as social interaction. London: Sage.
[76] Faure, A. M. 1996. The electoral system. Journal of theoretical politics, 8 (2): 193 - 208.
[77] Flowerdew, J. 1997. The discourse of colonial withdrawal: A case study in the creation of mythic discourse. Discourse and society, 8 (4): 517 - 593.
[78] Flowerdew, J. 1998. The final years of British Hong Kong: The discourse of colonial withdrawal. London: Macmillan.
[79] Flowerdew, J. 2002. The discourse of globalization: A view from the east. Discourse and society, 12 (2): 209 - 225.
[80] Flowerdew, J. 2004a. Identity politics and Hong Kong's return to Chinese

sovereignty: Analyzing the discourse of Hong Kong's first Chief Executive. Journal of pragmatics, (36): 1551 - 1578.

[81] Flowerdew, J. 2004b. The discursive construction of a world-class city. Discourse and society, 15 (5): 578 - 605.

[82] Fowler, R. & Kress, G. 1979. Rules and regulations. In Fowler, R. (ed.), Language and control. London: Routledge.

[83] Fowler, R. 1991. Language in the news. London: Routledge.

[84] Frege, G. 1892. On Sinn and Bedeutung. In Frege, 1897. Oxford: Basil Blackwell.

[85] Frow, J. 1986. Marxism and literary history. Oxford: Blackwell.

[86] Fühlau, I. 1982. Die Sprachlosigkeit der Inhaltsanalyse. Linguistische bemerkungen zu einer sozialwissenschaftlichen analyse. Tübingen.

[87] Fung, A. 2008. Discourse and cultural identity: Towards a global identity for Hong Kong. In Wu, D. (ed), Discourses of cultural China in the globalizing age. Hong Kong: Hong Kong University Press.

[88] Gee, J. P. 1998. What is literacy? In V. Zamel & R. Spack (eds.), Negotiating academic literacies: Teaching and learning across languages and cultures. Mahwah, New Jersey: Erlbaum.

[89] Gee, J. P. 2005. An introduction to discourse analysis: Theory and method. London, New York: Routledge.

[90] Geis, M. 1987. The language of politics. New York: Springer-Verlag.

[91] Hall, S. 1996a. The question of cultural identity. In Hall, S., Held, D., Hubert, D. & Thompson, K. (eds.), Modernity: An introduction to modern societies. Blackwell, MA, Cambridge.

[92] Hall, S. 1996b. Introduction: Who needs "Identity"? In Hall, S. & Du Gay, Paul (eds.), Questions of cultural identity. London, Thousand Oaks and New Delhi: 1 - 17.

[93] Halliday, M. A. K. 1978. Language as social semiotic: The social interpretation of language and meaning. London: Edward Arnold.

[94] Halliday, M. A. K. 1994. An introduction to functional grammar. London: Edward Arnold.

[95] Halliday, M. A. K. & Hasan, R. (eds.) 1989. Language, context and text: Aspects of language in a social-semiotic perspective. Oxford: Oxford University Press.

[96] Halliday, M. A. K. & Martin, J. R. 1993. Writing science. Literacy and discursive power. London: The Falmer Press.
[97] Halliday, M. A. K. & Matthiessen, C. 2004. An introduction to functional grammar. London: Edward Arnold.
[98] Halliday, M. A. K. & Mathiessen, C. 1999. Construing experience through meaning: A language-based approach to cognition. London: Cassell.
[99] Harris, Z. 1952. Discourse analysis. Language, 28: 474 –494.
[100] Hasan, R. 1996. Literacy, everyday talk and society In Hasan, R & Williams, G. (eds) . Literacy in society. London: Longman.
[101] Herman, E. S. & Chomsky, N. 1988. Manufacturing consent: The political economy of the mass media. New York: Pantheon.
[102] Hobbs, P. 2003. Is that what we're here about: A lawyer's use of impression management in a closing argument at trial. Discourse and society, 14 (3): 273 –290.
[103] Huang, Y. 2007. Pragmatics. Oxford: Oxford University Press.
[104] Ivanic, R. 1998. Writing and identity: The discoursal construction of identity in academic writing. Amsterdam, philadelphia: John Benjamins.
[105] Januschek, F. 1994 J. Haider und der rechtspopulistische Diskurs in Osterreich. In G. Tributsch (ed), S. Haider. Ein politisches lexicon seiner Ausspruche von 1986 bis heute. Vienna: Falter Verlag.
[106] Jaworski, A. & Coupland, N. (eds.) 1999. The discourse reader. London: Routledge.
[107] Johnstone, B. 2002. Discourse analysis. Oxford: Blackwell.
[108] Joseph, J. 2004. Procedural politics: Issues, influence and institutional choice in the European union. Cambridge: Cambridge University Press.
[109] Kammerer, O. 1995. Strassburg-das Selbstverständnis einer Stadt im 13. Jahrhundert. In H. Wilfried (Hg.), Europas Städte zwischen Zwang und Freiheit. Die europäische Stadt um die Mittedes 13. Jahrhunderts. Universitäts Verlag Regensburg, Regensburg.
[110] Kellett, E. E. 1969. Literary quotation and allusion. Port Washington, New York: Kennikat Press.
[111] Kress, G. & Hodge, B. 1979. Language as ideology. London: Routledge.
[112] Kress, G. 1989. Linguistic processes in socio-cultural practice. Oxford: Oxford University Press.

[113] Kristeva, J. 1986. Word, dialogue and novel. In Moi, T. (ed.), The Kristeva reader. Oxford: Blackwell.

[114] Krzyzanowski, M. 2005. European identity wanted! On discursive dimensions of European Convention. In R. Wodak and P. Chilton (eds.), New research agenda in CDA: Theory and multi-disciplinarity. Amsterdam, Philadelphia: John Benjamins

[115] Labov, W. 1963. The social motivation of a sound change. Word, 19: 273 – 309.

[116] Lalouschek, J., Menz, F. & Wodak, R. 1990. Alltag in der Ambulanz. Gesprache Zwischen Arzten, Schwestern und Patienten. Narr: Tubingen.

[117] Lau, N. K. 2001. Tung sticks to Confucian way. South China morning post, February 29.

[118] Lau, N. K. 2002. Chief persists in trying to run city-state as a company. South China morning post, February 29.

[119] Lau, S. K. 1997. 'Hongkongese' or 'Chinese': Hong Kong Chinese's identity, 1985 – 1995, Twenty-first Century.

[120] Lee, Martin, 2002. Listen to us and learn, Mr. Tung. South China morning post, February 2.

[121] Lemke, J. L. 1983. Thematic analysis: Systems, structures, and strategies. Semiotic enquiry, 3 (2): 159 – 187.

[122] Lemke, J. L. 1985. Ideology, intertexuality and the notion of reister. In D. James, B. & William, S. G. (eds.), Systematic perspectives on discourse, volume 1. Norwood, New Jersey: Ablex.

[123] Lemke, J. L. 1988a. Discourse in conflict: Heteroglossia and text semantics. In J. D. Benson & W. S. Greaves (eds.), Systemic functional approaches to discourse. Norwood, New Jersey: Ablex.

[124] Lemke, J. L. 1988b. Text structure and text semantics. In R. Veltman & E. Steiner (eds.), Pragmatics, discourse, and text. London: Pinter.

[125] Lemke, J. L. 1995a. Intertextuality and text semantics. In P. Fries & M. Gregory (eds.), Discourse in society: Systemic functional perspectives: Meaning and choice in language: Studies for Michael Halliday. Norwood, New Jersey: Ablex.

[126] Lemke, J. L. 1995b. Textual politics: Discourse and social dynamics. London: Taylor and Francis Ltd.

[127] Leppihalme, R. 1994. Translity allusions: When minimal change is not enough. Target: International Journal of Translation Studies, 6 (2): 177 - 193.

[128] Leung, A. 2002. Tung stays true to the electorate that counts most. South China morning post, February 26.

[129] Levinson, S. C. 1983. Pragmatics. Cambridge: Cambridge University Press.

[130] Luke, A. 2002. Beyond science and ideology critique: Developments in critical discourse analysis. Annual review of applied linguistics, 22: 96 - 110.

[131] Ma & Fung, 1999. Re-scinicization, nationalism and the Hong Kong identity. In So, C. & Chen, J. (eds.), Press and politics in Hong Kong: Case studies from 1967 to 1997. Hong Kong: Chinese University Press.

[132] Ma, K. W., Lui, T. L. & Ng, C. H. (eds). 1999. Cultural politics in Hong Kong. Hong Kong: Oxford University Press.

[133] Maingueneau, D. 1987. Nouvelles tendances en analyse du discours. Paris: Hachette.

[134] Martin, J. R. 1992. English text: System and structure. Amsterdam Philadelphia: John Benjamins.

[135] Martin, D. C. 1995. The choice of identity. Social identities, 1 (1): 5 - 20.

[136] Martin, J. R. 2000. Beyond exchange: Appraisal systems in English. In S. Hunston & G. Thompson. (eds), Evaluation in Text: Authorial Stance and the Construction of Discourse. Oxford: Oxford University Press.

[137] Martin, J. R. 2001. Language, register and genre. In A. Burns & C. Coffin (eds.), Analysing English in a Global Context: A Reader. London, New York: Continnum.

[138] Martin, J. R. & Rose, D. 2003. Working with discourse: Meaning beyond the clause. London, New York: Continnum.

[139] Mayring, P. 1983. Qualitative inhalts analyse. Grundlagen und Techniken. Basel: Beltz.

[140] Mead, G. H. 1967. Mind, self, and society from the standpoint of a social behaviorist. Chicago: Chicago University Press.

[141] Mey, J. 2001. Pragmatics: An introduction. Oxford: Blackwell.

[142] Meyer, M. 2001. Between theory, method, and politics: Positioning of

the approaches to CDA. In R. Wodak. & M. Meyer. (eds.), Methods of critical discourse analysis. London: Sage.

[143] Mills, S. 1997. Discourse. London: Routledge.

[144] Mitten, R. 1992. The politics of anti-semitic predudice: The Waldheim Phenomenon in Austria. Boulder, Barky Publishing Inc.

[145] Meinhof, U. & Smith, J. (eds.) 2000. Intertextuality and the media. From genre to everyday life. Manchester: Manchester University Press.

[146] Milroy, L. 1980. Language and social network. Oxford: Blackwell.

[147] Mukarovsky, J. 1964. Standard language and poetic language. In Paul, L. G. (ed. and trans), A Prague School Reader on aesthetics, literary structure and style. Washington D. C.: Georgetown University Press.

[148] Muntigl, P., Weiss, G. & Wodak, R. (eds.). 2000. European Union discourse on un/employment. An interdisciplinary approach to employment policy-making and organizational change. Philadephia, Amsterdam: John Benjamins.

[149] Nadel, A. 1982. Translating the past: Literary allusions as covert criticism. The Georgia review, 36 (3): 639 –651.

[150] O'Halloran, K. 2003. Critical discourse analysis and language cognition. Edinburgh: Edinburgh University Press.

[151] O'Keefe, D. J. 2002. Persuasion: Theory & research. Thousand Oaks, CA: Sage.

[152] O'Toole, F. 1997. The Ex-isle of Erin: Emigration and Irish culture. In Mac Laughlin, J. (ed). Location and dislocation in contemporary Irish society: Emigration and Irish identities. Cork: Cork University Press.

[153] Oktar, L. 2001. The ideological organization of representational processes in the presentation of us and them. Discourse and society, 12 (3): 313 –346.

[154] Peheux, M. 1982. Language, semantics and ideology. London: Macmillan.

[155] Paier, G. 1996. Menschen im Übergang. Österreichbilder und nationale Identität von Ex-und NeoösterreicherInnen. In H. Max Identität und Nationalstolz der Österreicher. Gesellschaftliche Ursachen und Funktionen. Böhlau Verlag: Wien-Köln-Weimar.

[156] Partington, A. 2003. The linguistics of political argument: The spin-doctor and the wolf-pack at the White House. London, New York: Routledge.

[157] Pelinka, A. & Wodak, R. 2002. Politik der Ausgrentzung. Vienna: Czernin

Verlag.

[158] Pennycook, A. 1994. Incommensurable discourse? Applied Linguistics, 15 (2): 115 - 137.

[159] Pennycook, A. 2001. Critical applied linguistics: A critical introduction. London: Erlbaum.

[160] Perri, C. 1978. On alluding. Poetics, 7: 289 - 307.

[161] Pfeiffer, H., Wunderlich, S., Bender, W., Elz, U. & Horn, B. 1987. Music improvisation with schizophrenic patients—A controlled study in the assessment of therapeutic effects. Rehabilitation stuttgart, 26: 184 - 192.

[162] Rathzel, N. 1994. Harmonious "Heimat" and Disturbing "Auslander". In K. K. Bhavani & A. Phoenix, (eds), Shifting indentities and shifting racisms. Phoenix. London: Sage.

[163] Reisigl, M. 2004. 'Wie man eine Nation herbeiredet. Eine diskursanalytische Untersuchung zur sprachlichen Konstruktion österreichischen Nation und österreichischen Identität in politischen Fest-und Gedenkreden', PhD thesis, University of Vienna.

[164] Reisigl, M. & Wodak, R. 2001. Discourse and discrimination. Rhetorics of racism and antisemitism. London: Routledge.

[165] Renkema, J. 2004. Introduction to discourse studies. Amsterdam, Philadelphia: John Benjamins.

[166] Ricento. 2003. The discursive construction of Americanism. Discourse and society, 14 (5).

[167] Ricceur, P. 1992. Oneself as another. Chicago: University of Chicago Press.

[168] Sandig, B. 1986. Textwissen. Beschreibungsmoglichkeiten und Realisierungen von Textmustern am Beispiel der Richtigstellung. In E. Engelkamp E. (eds.) Wissensreprasentation und Wissensaustausch. St. Ingbert: Rohrig.

[169] Schegloff, E. A. 1997. Whose text? Whose context? Discourse and society, 8 (2): 165 - 187.

[170] Schiffrin, D. 1994. Approaches to discourse. Oxford: Blackwell.

[171] Schwartz, M. N. K. & Flammer, A. 1981. Text structure and title—Effects on comprehension and recall. Journal of verbal learning and verbal behaviour, 20: 61 - 66.

[172] Scollon, R. 1998. Mediated discourse as social interaction: A study of news discourse. London: Longman.

[173] Scollon, R. 1999. Official and unofficial discourses of national identity: Questions raised by the case of contemporary Hong Kong. In R. Wodak & C Ludwig (eds), Challenges in a changing world: Issues in critical discourse analysis. Vienna: Passagen Berlag.

[174] Scollon, R. 2000. Methodological interdiscursivity: An ethnographic understanding of unfinalisability. In Sarange, S. & M. Coulthard (eds.), Discourse and social life. London: Pearson Education Limited.

[175] Scollon, R. 2002. Interdiscursivity and identity. In M. Toolan (ed.), Critical discourse analysis: Critical concepts in linguistics. London: Routledge.

[176] Scollon, R. 2004. Intertextuality across communities of practice: Academics, journalism and advertising. In C. L. Moder & A. Martinovic-Zic (eds.), Discourse across languages and cultures. Amsterdam, Philadelphia: John Benjamins.

[177] Scollon, R., Bhatia, V., Li, D. & Yung, V. 1999. Blurred genres and fuzzy identities in Hong Kong public discourse: Foundational ethnographic issues. Applied linguistics, 20 (1): 22 –43.

[178] Scollon, R. & Scollon, S. 1997. Political, personal, and commercial discourses of national sovereignty: Hong Kong becomes China. In M. Lauristin (ed.), Intercultural communication and changing national identities. Tartu: Tartu University Press.

[179] Scollon, R. & Scollon, S. 2004. Nexus analysis: Discourse and the emerging Internet. London: Routledge.

[180] Scollon, S. 2000. Political and somatic alignment: habitus, ideology and social practice. Paper given at the workshop on Theory and Interdisciplinarity in Critical Discourse Analysis, Institute on Discourse, Identity and Politics, University of Vienna.

[181] Scott, M. & Tribble, C. 2006. Textual patterns. Key words and corpus analysis in language education. Amsterdam, Philadelphia: Benjamins.

[182] Searle, J. R. 1969. Speech acts: An essay in the philosophy of language. Cambridge: Cambridge University Press. Searle, J. R. 1976. Indirect speech acts. In P. Cole and Morgan, J. (eds.), Syntax

and semantics 3: speech acts. New York: Academic Press.
[183] Sheyholislami, J. 2001. Critical Discourse Analysis. Retrieved from: http: // www. carleton. ca/ ~jsheyhol/cda. htm.
[184] Soames, S. 1989. Presupposition. In Gabbay & Guenthner (eds.), Handbook of philosophical logic.
[185] Sperber, D. & Wilsons, D. 1986. Relevance: Communication and cognition. Oxford: Blackwell.
[186] Strawson, P. 1950. Introduction to logical theory. London: Methuen.
[187] Strawson, P. 1950. On referring, mind 59. Reprinted in P. F. Strawson London: Methuen.
[188] Stubbs, M. 1996. Text and corpus analysis: Computer-assisted studies of language and culture. Oxford: Blackwell. Stubbs, M. 1997. Whorf's Children: Critical comments on Critical Discourse Analysis (CDA). In A. Ryan & A. Wray (eds.), Evolving models of language. Clevedon: BAAL in association with Multilingual Matters.
[189] Teubert, W. 2000. Starting with trauer: Approaches to multilingual lexical semantics. In papers in computational lexicography complex'99, F. Kiefer, G. Kiss & J. Pajzs (eds). Budapest: Linguistics Institute, Hungarian Academy of Sciences.
[190] Titscher, S. et al. 1998. Methoden der Textanalyse. Leitfaden und Uberblick: Opladen.
[191] Threadgold, T. 2003. Cultural studies, Critical theory and critical discourse analysis: Histories, remembering and futures. Linguistik Online. Vol. 114. Retrieved from: http: /www. Linguistic-online. de.
[192] Toolan, M. 1997. What is critical discourse analysis and why are people saying such terrible things about it? Language and literature, 6 (2): 83 – 103.
[193] Toolan, M. (ed.) 2002. Critical discourse analysis. Critical concepts in linguistics. London: Routledge.
[194] Trew, T. 1979. What the papers say: Linguistic variation and ideological difference. In R. Fowler, R. Hodge, G. Kress & T. Trew (eds), Language and control. London: Routledge.
[195] van Dijk, T. A. 1988b. News analysis: Case studies of international and national news in the press. Hillsdale, New Jersey: Erlbaum.
[196] van Dijk, T. A. 1991. Media contents. The interdisciplinary study of news

as discourse. In Bruhn-Jensen, K. and Jankowksi, N. (eds.), Handbook of qualitative methods in mass communication research. London: Routledge, pp.

[197] van Dijk, T. A. 1993. Discourse and cognition in society. In D. Crowley & D. Mitchell (eds.), Communication theory today. Oxford: Pergamon Press.

[198] van Dijk, T. A. 1995. Ideological discourse analysis. In E. Ventola & A. Solin (eds.), Special issue: Interdisciplinary approaches to discourse analysis in new courant 4. Helsinki: University of Helsinki.

[199] van Dijk, T. A. 1996. Discourse, opinions and ideologies. In Schaffner, C., Kelly-Holmes, H. (eds.), Discourse and ideologies. Bristol: Multilingual Matters Ltd.

[200] van Dijk, T. A. (ed.) 1997. Discourse studies: A multidisciplinary introduction. London: Sage.

[201] van Dijk, T. A. 1998a. Ideology: A multidisciplinary approach. London: Sage.

[202] van Dijk, T. A. 1998b. News as discourse. Hillsdale, New Jersey: Erlbaum.

[203] van Dijk, T. A. 1999. Critical discourse analysis and conversation analysis. Discourse and society, 10 (4): 459-480.

[204] van Dijk, T. A. 2001. Discourse, ideology and context. Folia linguistica, 35 (1-2): 11-40.

[205] van Dijk, T. A. 2002. Political discourse and political cognition. In P. A. Chilton & C. Schafner (eds.), Politics as text and talk: Analytic approaches to political discourse. Amsterdam, Philadelphia: John Benjamins.

[206] van Dijk, T. A. 2003. The discourse-knowledge interface. In G. Weisis & R. Wodak (eds.), Critical discourse analysis: Theory and interdisciplinarity. New York: Palgrave Macmillan.

[207] van Dijk, T. A. 2004. Macro context. First International Conference on discourse and intercultural relations. University of Murcia, 23 - 25. September, 2004.

[208] van Dijk, T. A. 2005. Contextual knowledge management in discourse production: A CDA perspective. In Wodak, R. and Chilton, P. (eds.),

New agenda in (Critical) discourse analysis. Amsterdam, Philadelphia: Benjamins.

[209] van Dijk, T. A. 2006a. Discourse, context and cognition. Discourse studies, 8 (1): 159 – 177.

[210] van Dijk, T. A. 2006b. Discourse and manipulation. Discourse and society, 17 (3): 359 – 383.

[211] van Dijk, T. A. & Kintsh, W. 1983. Strategies of discourse comprehension. London: Academic Press.

[212] van Leeuwen, T. 1993. Genre and field in critical discourse analysis. Discourse and society, 4 (2): 193 – 223.

[213] van Leeuwen, T. 1995. Representing social action. Discourse and society, 6 (1): 81 – 106.

[214] van Leeuwen, T. 1996. The representation of social actors. In Texts and Practices: Readings in Critical Discourse Analysis C. R. Caldas-Coulthard & M. Coulthard. London: Routtedge, pp. 32 – 70.

[215] van Leeuwen, T. & Wodak, R. 1999. Legitimizing immigration control: A discourse-historical analysis, Valencia, 5 May.

[216] van Leeuwen, T. 2005. Introducing social semiotics. London: Routledge.

[217] Var Der Valk, I. 2003. Right-wing parliamentary discourse on immigration in France. Discourse and society, 14 (3): 309 – 348.

[218] Volmert, J. 1989. Politische Rhetorik des Nationalsozialismus. In E. Konrad (ed.), Sprache im Faschismus, Frankfurt am Main, 137 – 161.

[219] Weiss, G, & Wodak, R. 2003. Intruduction: Theory, interdisciplinarity and critical discourse analysis. In Weiss, G. & Wodak, R. (eds.), Critical discourse analysis: Theory and interdisciplinarity. New York: Palgrave Macmillan.

[220] West, C. 1990. Not just 'doctors' orders': Directive—response sequences in patients' visits to women and men physicians. Discourse and society, 1: 85 – 112.

[221] Wetherell, M. 1998. Positioning and interpretative repertoires: Conversation analysis and post-structuralism in dialogue. Discourse and society, 9: 387 – 412.

[222] White, P. R. 2002. Appraisal—the language of evaluation and stance. In J. Verschueren, Jan-J. O. Ostman, J. Blommaert & C. Bulcaen, (eds.),

Handbook of pragmatics. Amsterdam, Philadelphia: John Benjamins.
[223] Widdowson, H. G. 1995. Norman Fairclough: Discourse and social change. Applied linguistics, 16 (4): 510 – 516.
[224] Widdowson, H. G. 1998. The theory and practice of critical discourse analysis. Applied linguistics, 19 (1): 136 – 151.
[225] Wilson, J. 1990. Politically speaking: The pragmatic analysis of political language. Oxford: Blackwell.
[226] Wilson, J. 2001. Political discourse. In D. Schiffrin, D. Tannen, & H. E. Hamilton (eds.), The handbook of discourse analysis. Malden, MA: Blackwell Publishers Inc.
[227] Wilss, W. 1989. Anspielungen: Zur Manifestation Von Kreativitat und Routine in der Sprachverwendung. Tubinger: Max Niemeyer Verlag.
[228] Wodak, R., P. Nowak, J. Pelikan, H. Gruber, R. de Cillia, & R. Mitten, 1990. Wir sind alle unschuldige Tater! Diskurshistorische Studien zum Nachkriegsantisemitismus Frankfurt/M.: Suhrkamp.
[229] Wodak. R. 1995. Critical linguistics and critical discourse analysis. In J. Verschueren, J. Ostman, & J. Bloomaert (eds). Handbook of pragmatics. Amsterdam, Philadelphia: John Benjamins.
[230] Wodak, R. (ed.) 1996. Disorders of discourse. London: Longman.
[231] Wodak, R. (ed.) 1997. Gender and discourse. London: Sage.
[232] Wodak, R. 1998. Critical discourse analysis at the end of the 20th century. Research on language and social interaction, 32: 185 – 194.
[233] Wodak, R. & Ludwig, C. (ed.). 1999. Challenges in a changing world: Issues in critical discourse analysis. Vienna: Passagenverlag.
[234] Wodak, R. 2000. Sociolinguistics: Does it need a social theory? New perspectives in critical discourse analysis. Discourse and society, 2 (3): 123 – 147.
[235] Wodak, R. 2001. What CDA is about: A summary of its history, important concepts and its developments. In R. Wodak & M. Meyer (eds.), Methods of critical discourse analysis. London: Sage.
[236] Wodak, R. 2004. Pupolist discourse: The Austrian case. In Rydgren, J. (ed.), Moments of exclusion: radical right-wing populism. London: Nova Science Publishers Inc.
[237] Wodak, R. 2006. Images in/and news in a globalized world. In Larsen,

I. , Strunck, J. & Verstergaard, T. (eds.), Mediating ideology in text and image. Amsterdam, Philadelphia: John Benjamins.

[238] Wodak, R. 2007b. Pragmatics and critical discourse analysis: A cross-disciplinary inquiry. Pragmatics & cognition, 15 (1): 203 - 225.

[239] Wodak, R. 2007a. Language and ideology—Language in ideology. Journal of language and politics, 6 (1): 1 - 5.

[240] Wodak, R, et al. 2008. A Useful methodological synergy? Combining critical discourse analysis and corpus linguistics to examine discourses of refugees and asylum seekers in the UK press. Discourse and society, 19 (3): 273 - 306.

[241] Wodak, R., de Cilla, R., Reisigl, M. & Liebhart, K. 1999. The discursive construction of national identity (A. Hirsch & R. Mitten, trans.). Edinburgh: Edinburgh University Press.

[242] Wodak. R. & Meyer, M. (eds.). 2001. Methods of critical discourse analysis. London: Sage.

[243] Wodak, R. & Weiss, G. 2005. Analyzing European Union discourses: theories and applications. In Wodak R. & Chilton P. (eds.), A new agenda in (Critical) discourse analysis. London: John Benjamins.

[244] Wong, R. 1999. In-between nationalism and colonialism: Constructing Hong Kong Chinese identities in the development of China. PhD dissertation.

[245] Wong T. K. 1996. Priming and election: An analysis of the 1995 Legislative Council Election. In Kuan, H. C, et al. The 1995 legislative council election in Hong Kong. Hong Kong: Hong Kong Institute of Asian-Pacific Studies, The Chinese University of Hong Kong.

[246] Woodward, K. 1997. Identity and difference. London: Sage.

[247] Yeung, C. 1997. A new and maybe better Hong Kong is on the horizon, but there's a price that has to be paid; Why Tung must build with care. South China morning post, October 11.

[248] Yeung, C. 1998. Role of civil servants comes under scrutiny. South China morning post, July 1.

[249] Yeung, C. 1999. Haunted by the municipal councils. South China morning post, December 30.

[250] Yeung, C. 2001. One country, multitude of problems. South China

morning post, December 30.

[251] Yeung, C. 2002. Here's to reform, Mr Tung. South China morning post. Feb. 22.

[252] Yeung, C. & Cheung, J. 2002. Democracy drive disappoints. South China morning post, June 3.

[253] Yeung, Y. 1998. Globalization and the world of large cities. New York: University Press.

[254] Yule, G. 1996. Pragmatics. Oxford: Oxford University Press.

[255] 陈建平，王加林．互文性与身份建构话语策略．中国外语，2014（1）.

[256] 彭庆．从政府工作报告的文字表述看我国多边外交政策：1986—2005. 外交评论，2005（8）.

[257] 王加林，戈军．语言政策与身份建构．社会科学家，2012（1）.

[258] 王加林，贺显斌．回归前后香港施政报告中 WE 的使用与香港人身份的建构．解放军外国语学院学报，2012（3）.

[259] 王加林，李玉坤．回归前后香港政府施政报告内容分析的对比研究．广东外语外贸大学学报，2013（5）.

[260] 王加林，申智奇．语用预设与香港人身份的话语构建．天津外国语大学学报，2016（5）.

[261] 辛斌．批评语言学：理论与应用．上海：上海外语教育出版社，2005.

[262] 尤泽顺，陈建平．话语秩序与对外政策构建：对《政府工作报告》的词汇变化分析．广东外语外贸大学学报，2009（2）.

[263] 郑华．从话语分析看布什访华．国际论坛，2006（8）.

# Appendix

22 Policy Addresses in the present research

1. 1986 Policy Address delivered by Sir Edward Youde.
2. 1987 Policy Address delivered by Sir David Wilson.
3. 1988 Policy Address delivered by Sir David Wilson.
4. 1989 Policy Address delivered by Sir David Wilson.
5. 1990 Policy Address delivered by Sir David Wilson.
6. 1991 Policy Address delivered by Sir David Wilson.
7. 1992 Policy Address delivered by Christopher Francis Patten.
8. 1993 Policy Address delivered by Christopher Francis Patten.
9. 1994 Policy Address delivered by Christopher Francis Patten.
10. 1995 Policy Address delivered by Christopher Francis Patten.
11. 1996 Policy Address delivered by Christopher Francis Patten.

The above 11 Policy Addresses were obtained from the Chongji Library of Chinese University of Hong Kong.

The following 11 Policy Addresses were obtained from the website:
http://www.policyaddress.gov.hk/

12. 1997 Policy Address delivered by Tung Chee-hwa (Dong Jianhua).
13. 1998 Policy Address delivered by Tung Chee-hwa (Dong Jianhua).
14. 1999 Policy Address delivered by Tung Chee-hwa (Dong Jianhua).
15. 2000 Policy Address delivered by Tung Chee-hwa (Dong Jianhua).
16. 2001 Policy Address delivered by Tung Chee-hwa (Dong Jianhua).
17. 2003 Policy Address delivered by Tung Chee-hwa (Dong Jianhua).
18. 2004 Policy Address delivered by Tung Chee-hwa (Dong Jianhua).
19. 2005 Policy Address delivered by Donald Tsang Yam-kuen.

20. 2006 Policy Address delivered by Donald Tsang Yam-kuen.
21. 2007 Policy Address delivered by Donald Tsang Yam-kuen.
22. 2008 Policy Address delivered by Donald Tsang Yam-kuen.